# THE HACKABLE CITY:
## A RESEARCH MANIFESTO AND DESIGN TOOLKIT

Cristina Ampatzidou, Matthijs Bouw, Froukje van de Klundert, Michiel de Lange, Martijn de Waal

# COLOPHON

The Hackable City: A Research Manifesto and Design Toolkit

**Authors**
Cristina Ampatzidou (University of Amsterdam / University of Groningen)
Matthijs Bouw (One Architecture)
Froukje van de Klundert (University of Amsterdam)
Michiel de Lange (Utrecht University)
Martijn de Waal (Amsterdam University of Applied Sciences / University of Amsterdam)

**Design** UNDOG, Amsterdam
**EPUB development** Jess van Zyl
**Copy-editor** Russell Kinch
**Printer** Offsetdrukkerij Nuance, Zaandam
**Publisher** Amsterdam Creative Industries Publishing, Rose Leighton
**Supported by** Amsterdam University of Applied Sciences (Hogeschool van Amsterdam), PublishingLab
**Cover image** Marc Faasse (www.ndsm.nl/speeltuin)
**Photography** Marc Faasse, Michiel de Lange, Pink Pony Express
**Diagrams** Juliette Sung

**Contact** Amsterdam Creative Industries Publishing, www.amsterdamcreativeindustries.com

EPUB and PDF editions of this publication are freely downloadable from our website, www.publishinglab.nl/publications

This publication is licensed under Creative Commons Attribution-NonCommercial-ShareAlike 4.0 International (CC-BY-NC-SA 4.0)

Amsterdam, December 2015

**ISBN** 978-94-92171-04-7 (print)
**ISBN** 978-94-92171-05-4 (ePub)

# CONTENTS

Introduction: the Rise of the Platform Society ................................................................. 11
A Hackable City Research Manifesto ............................................................................... 17
The Hackable City Toolkit .................................................................................................. 31
Case Studies ....................................................................................................................... 51
Further Thoughts ................................................................................................................ 69

## ACKNOWLEDGEMENTS

The Hackable City is a research project on the role of digital media in the process of citymaking that resulted from a cooperation between One Architecture and The Mobile City Foundation. The project investigates the opportunities of digital media technologies for the empowerment of citizens and other stakeholders in a democratic process of citymaking. It also explores the shift in roles of and relationships between governments, (design) professionals and citizens in this process.

The first contours for this project were laid out by One Architecture and The Mobile City during the Metropool NL workshop organized by the Deltametropool Society in 2012, resulting in the publication *Eindhoven, Hackable World City*. This was followed by an 'embedded researcher' project hosted at the University of Amsterdam and One Architecture and funded by the Creative Industries Research Centre Amsterdam, with contributions from Utrecht University. In 2014, funding was received from the Netherlands Organization for Scientific Research (NWO) for both a KIEM-exploration through Utrecht University and a Creative Industries research project hosted at the University of Amsterdam (UvA), The Amsterdam University of Applied Sciences (AUAS), and One Architecture. For the latter, new partners joined the research coalition: The Ministry of the Interior and Kingdom Relations, Pakhuis de Zwijger, and Stadslab Buiksloterham.

**Current Research Team** Matthijs Bouw (Researcher, Director One Architecture); Tara Karpinski (Embedded Researcher, University of Amsterdam & One Architecture); Froukje van de Klundert (Embedded Researcher, University of Amsterdam); Michiel de Lange (Researcher, Utrecht University); Karel Millenaar (Designer, AUAS); Martijn de Waal (Project leader, UvA / AUAS).

**Board of Advisors** Ger Baron (Chief Technology Officer, City of Amsterdam); Coby van Berkum (Chair Administrative Council, Amsterdam-Noord); Guus Beumer (Director, Het Nieuwe Instituut); José van Dijck (Professor Comparative Media Studies, University of Amsterdam); Egbert Fransen (Director, Pakhuis de Zwijger); Maarten Hajer (distinguished professor Urban Futures, Utrecht University); Freek van 't Ooster (Director, Immovator); Ben Schouten (Lector Play & Civic Media, Amsterdam University of Applied Sciences); Mildo van Staden (Senior Advisor, Ministry of the Interior and Kingdom Relations).

www.thehackablecity.nl / info@thehackablecity.nl

## DEFINITIONS

**The Hackable City** (normative definition):
In a hackable city, new media technologies are employed to open up urban institutions and infrastructures to systemic change in the public interest. It combines top-down smart-city technologies with bottom-up 'smart citizen' initiatives.
In a hackable city, the urban (data) infrastructure functions as a platform that can be appropriated and incrementally improved upon by various stakeholders.

**The Hackable City** (research project):
The goal of this research project is to explore the opportunities as well as challenges of the rise of new media technologies for an open, democratic process of collaborative citymaking. How can citizens, design professionals, local government institutions and others employ digital media platforms in collaborative processes of urban planning, management and social organization, to contribute to a liveable and resilient city, with a strong social fabric?

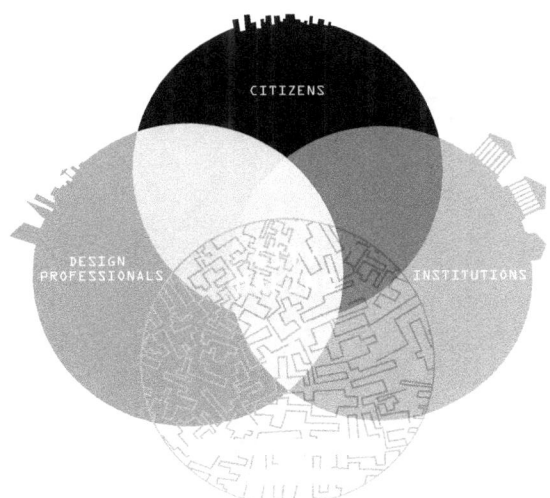

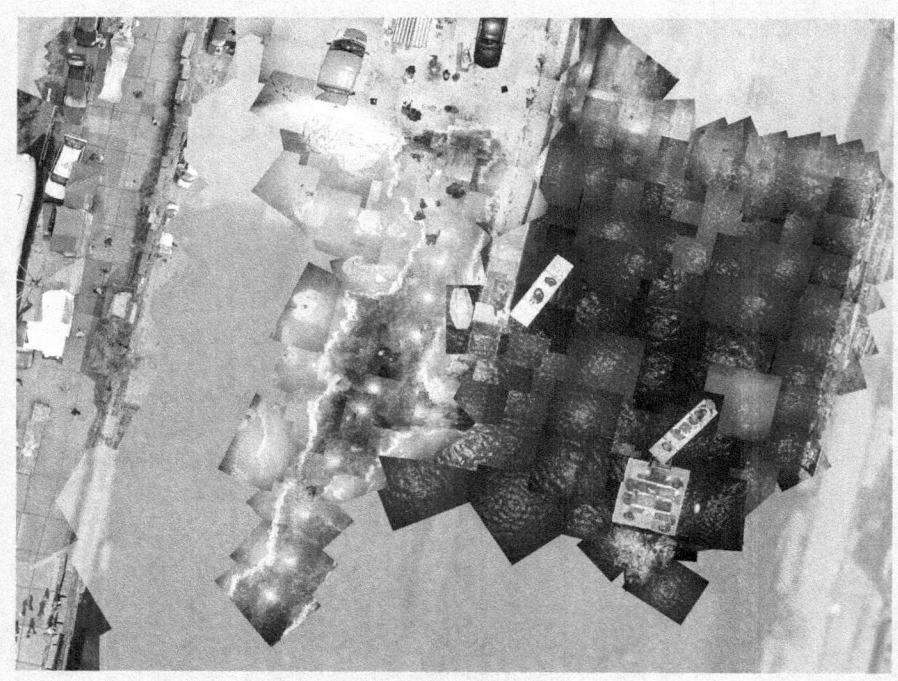

# INTRODUCTION: THE RISE OF THE PLATFORM SOCIETY

For citymakers all around the world, we live in interesting times, full of paradoxes. Whereas local governments are teaming up with technology companies to make their cities 'smarter' and turn them into living labs, citizen initiatives all over the world have started to emerge bottom-up around numerous issues, from collective neighborhood gardens to energy cooperatives. On the one hand, technology enthusiasts and entrepreneurs sing the praise of innovative approaches to transit, ranging from Uber to the advent of the driverless car. On the other, newspaper columns are filled with critical op-ed contributions addressing the negative consequences of the so-called sharing economy, varying from increasing pressure on already tight housing markets to subpar working conditions for those employed in the on-demand economy. Finally, while personalized services such as Google Maps, local restaurant review sites and sporting apps possibly provoke a shift towards a more individualistic experience of the city, a young generation of architects and designers is employing a series of digital platforms to crowdfund and crowdsource projects that are to revitalize public space, to contribute to a circular economy, or to build local communities or jumpstart a civic economy.

What binds these examples together is that they are part of an underlying shift in the organization of our societies, a shift that we could call 'the rise of the platform society' – a society in which more and more of our social and economic interactions are mediated through digital media platforms. Whether it's finding a taxi through Uber, arranging a date through Tinder, connecting with neighborhood-dwellers to collectively start a solar energy initiative or searching for fellow-enthusiasts to turn parking places into 'parklets' (small parks the size of a parking place), it seems that, as a current tech-commercial claimed: *there's an app for that*. Or at least a neighborhood blog, an Instructable-video, an online forum, a crowdsourcing tool, a social network, or any other kind of digital media platform that connects supply and demand in a broad variety of societal domains through its software.

This growing use of digital media platforms in our everyday urban culture has great consequences for what we call citymaking: the ways in which a broad variety of actors decide upon, design, program, manage and appropriate the physical city and its social life. To put it in the terminology of this research project: in the platform society it may become easier to 'hack' the existing fabric of our cities and appropriate it for our own uses, whether it's temporarily converting our apartment into a hotel, or mobilizing 'friends' at a public park - regardless whether it's for a communal bbq, a political rally or a riot against the powers that be. As a consequence, we may make use of our urban infrastructures in more efficient ways and find more flexible ways to program our cities, mobilize crowds, organize communities, activate places and negotiate transactions.

> In the platform society it may become easier
> to 'hack' the existing fabric of our cities and appropriate it for our own uses

Following the sometimes positivist swing to the rhetoric of the platform society, the connections these new platforms forge may empower citizens in new ways to organize themselves around all kind of issues, bringing about a sharing economy, a participation society or a civic economy. Yet, such a future is far from assured. As critics have pointed out, these very same developments – sometimes sold under the guise of the smart city - may also threaten to subsume all social relations under the functionalist and commercial 'city as a service' logic of technology companies, leading to an increase in inequality and the further advent of technocratic urban governance.

## HACKABLE CITY OPPORTUNITIES & CHALLENGES

This publication, consisting of a 'Hackable City Research Manifesto' and a 'Hackable City Toolkit', aims to offer an inroad to grasp these developments as well as a practical guide to act upon them: What opportunities, as well as challenges, does the rise of the platform society pose for an open, democratic process of collaborative citymaking? And how can citizens, design professionals, local government institutions and others creatively use digital media platforms in collaborative processes of urban planning, management and social organization, to contribute to a liveable and resilient city, with a strong social fabric?

These are of course big questions that do not allow for easy answers. Yet in the end it's these very questions that need to be addressed. What we propose is an iterative step-by-step approach, to explore the challenges and opportunities digital media afford for citymaking, and this report is our first iteration of this process.

To address our research questions, we have taken on the metaphor of hacking - which could be defined as the playful and clever appropriation of a system through a learning-by-doing approach, in a spirit of sharing and collaboration. We think this notion of hacking is a productive way to approach the process of citymaking in the era of the platform society. As it is a term derived from the world of computers and software, 'hacking' foregrounds the use of digital media platforms in the process. The notion of 'hacking', in the sense of 'opening up a system', connects with broader societal trends such as the rise of a civic or sharing economy, approaches of open innovation and collaborative planning, discussions about civic participation and the changing roles between experts and amateurs. How can we use these technologies to 'hack' (appropriate, adjust, extend, improve) the social, cultural and economic processes in our cities, from the perspective of the public interest?

As hacking addresses both the practices of the hacker as well as the logic of the system to be hacked, it also provides ways to overcome the current antagonism between top-down smart city developments (usually focussing on the system rather than its users) and bottom-up smart citizen initiatives (often focussing on the organization of citizens, sometimes overlooking its consequences for society as a whole). As such, the term also opens up a normative discussion that is of importance for designers, policy makers and citizens alike. To what extent can and should a city be 'hackable'? To whose advantage is a hackable city to be appropriated? How can we safeguard a public interest perspective when opening up the city for appropriation by a broad variety of actors? And how can we prevent criminal or socially destructive attempts to hack the city?

These last questions are important. As hacking also has a negative connotation, the use of this term also foregrounds the risks of the platform society. Whereas we use a positive definition of hacking, based on collaboration towards communal goals, hacking can also refer to criminals breaking into systems, stealing people's credit card numbers, endangering their privacy, or even bringing down vital computer systems by malicious attacks. Each technology can be used for contrarian purposes, and digital media platforms by their very nature are vulnerable to such attacks. Whereas in this study we are interested in the opportunities the platform society offers for more resilient, sustainable and sociable urban futures, the use of the very term hacking implies that design of such systems must always take these counter-attacks in mind. Privacy and safety of systems should not be an afterthought, but at the very heart of thinking about hackable cities.

As a last note, the verb hacking can also be understood as shorthand for a practical approach to solving complex issues. Hackers don't sit down to endlessly theorize, they just start patching up any problem with the means they happen to have at hand. Hacking is an iterative, learning-by-doing kind of process.

This research project follows a similar approach. Our manifesto and toolkit should be understood as a first probe, a beta-version, of our work in progress; work that may never be completely finished as technologies and conditions are continuously being updated as well. In the spirit of the hacker community: we nevertheless find it productive to share what we have put together so far, in the hope to spark a discussion and help others forward their research and design endeavours.

We will go about this as follows: In part I we will have a closer look at the implications of 'hackable city making' in the form of a Hackable City Research Manifesto. The goal of this Manifesto is to point out the main challenges and opportunities for a democratic process of citymaking in the emerging platform society. What new questions and approaches arise when we look at the process of citymaking through the lens of hackable city making? The manifesto is structured around eight Hackable City Research Questions, each of them addressing a particular aspect of the application of digital media technologies in the process of citymaking.

In part II we turn to the praxis of citymaking and exhibit a first 'beta-version' of a 'hackable city toolkit'. This toolkit could give designers, policy makers and citizens a number of ideas to approach projects that they might be working on, providing also a number of strategies to include in their projects. Learning from existing examples, we have identified a model that consists of seven phases that are addressed in the process of hackable citymaking. Furthermore, we have assembled the approaches we found in these phases into a toolkit of strategies. These tools will be further specified in the extensive descriptions of seven hackable city projects.
We hope that the Hackable City Research Manifesto in combination with the Hackable City Toolkit will give designers and community organizers (be they professionals or citizens themselves) a starting point to think about organizing their interventions, both from a philosophical and strategic as well as from a hands-on perspective. In a true hacker-approach, this toolkit should not be understood as an exhaustive or even prescriptive list, but as an inventory that may be hacked itself, and we welcome additions or alterations.

In the final chapter, we will conclude with a number of general reflections on the process of hackable citymaking. What points of further developing 'hackable city making' need our attention, both in research, design and policy?

# A HACKABLE CITY RESEARCH MANIFESTO

We have found the notion of hackability a useful lens to approach the increasing role of digital media in our urban societies, as well as to reflect on the changing relations between various parties in the process of citymaking. When looking at our cities through the lens of 'hacking', specific issues in the process of citymaking that need to be addressed suddenly become visible. At the same time, the ethos found in hacker communities that operate in the world of computers and software may give us interesting leads for the design and application of digital media platforms that contribute to open-ended, democratic and inclusive practices of citymaking.

To start our inquiry: as it is a term normally associated with the world of computers and software, the notion of hacking foregrounds the increasing role of software in our urban societies. As hacking can also mean 'breaking into systems' or 'bending the logic of systems', it also questions the openness of digital media platforms, and ultimately the cities they serve. To what extents can the logic of digital media platforms be bent or opened up for unforeseen purposes?

This is an important issue. After all, cities themselves have long been theorized as platforms, or 'market places' that in their various public, institutional and even private spaces connect supply and demand in numerous spheres. As Manuel Castells has argued, cities can be understood as material interfaces that connect individual city dwellers with collective practices, experiences and rhythms (Castells, 2002). In addition, it could be argued that the success of cities as economic and cultural systems has always depended on their 'hackability', or the ways in which their systematic workings can be (playfully) appropriated by its residents. That is: the force of cities is that they have been open systems whose infrastructure and overlapping social, cultural and economic networks can be put to use in new, unforeseen ways by a variety of actors. They are open platforms whose infrastructure and programme allow their residents to forge all kinds of linkages between them, contributing to both economic and cultural innovation as well as mutual trust between citizens. And although these activities are usually confined by what current laws allow for, cities have always remained open platforms where these laws can be challenged as well; be it through small scale tactical interventions or large revolutionary protest demonstrations.

·········
The force of cities is that they have been open systems whose infrastructure and overlapping social, cultural and economic networks can be put to use in new, unforeseen ways by a variety of actors
·········

What happens to these functions of the city now that in our everyday urban lives, we have started to make use of all kinds of digital interfaces to join supply and demand and to match individuals with collectives? Now that links are no longer forged by the overlapping spatial and social circuits of our everyday lives but through the algorithms of digital media platforms? Could this indeed empower citizens to organize themselves around all kinds of issues, forging new links and connections? Or, is it that, as other critics point out, these very same developments may also threaten to subsume all social relations under the commercial 'city as a service'- logic of technology companies that build the platforms through which our cities are organized? As some have pointed out, many current 'smart city' visions focus on the development of (usually) proprietary platforms that are to make the city more efficient. Among the issues that smart city policies seek to address are mobility, clean energy, water and food production and distribution, health, living and public participation (Hollands, 2008). Whereas that in itself could be a positive force, many of these visions have received wide criticism (see for example: Greenfield, 2013; Hemment & Townsend, 2013). By and large these criticisms have focussed on the ill-defined notion of "smartness" in smart city visions, targeted the simplified view of what cities actually are, and attacked their apolitical technocratic nature (see also Allwinkle & Cruickshank, 2011; Gabrys, 2014; Kitchin, 2013; Ratti & Townsend, 2011; Söderström, Paasche, & Klauser, 2014).

What does "smart" mean and who are actually supposed to be smart? Is city life and the urban experience about control, efficiency and predictability, or about encountering the unexpected and dealing with differences? Moreover, smart city views propose "technological fixes" to complex problems. Many so-called "smart technologies" or smart interventions are implicitly driven by a logic of consumption, control, and capsularization but do not empower citizens to become active players in their cities (de Lange & de Waal, 2013; Levy, 2001). The push for safety with CCTV and smart risk assessing algorithms could turn cities into places of pervasive control and surveillance. Smart retail solutions, location-based services and predictive algorithms push a consumerist view of urban life. And personal mobile technologies may foster a culture of capsularization and retreat. When technology-driven solutions ignore active contributions of citizens they may have adverse effects for urban public life at large.

The least that can be said in conclusion to these criticisms is that the software and interfaces of digital media platforms are not neutral tools for 'hacking the city'. They are an active actor, whose workings and design may reflect particular power structures or offer opportunities to revert these. Therefore, their logic should be understood by all parties involved in the process of citymaking, be they local governments, citizens or designers. Can citizens and other actors still hack into these systems, becomes an important question. To what extent do our cities remain the open systems that provided their success?

Hackable City Research Question 1
How can we safeguard the open character of our cities in the platform society?

## A BRIEF HISTORY OF HACKER CULTURE

The notion of 'hacking', or more precisely the hacker ethos found amongst a variety of tech- and computer-based subcultures labelled as such in the last half a century or so, may provide an answer to this first Hackable City Research Question. We argue that some of the values from these – by no means singular – subcultures could help us think about designing digital media platforms for 'open cities'. Or at least raise a set of relevant questions and issues to be tackled in the process. A somewhat closer look at this hacker's ethos will help to address these issues in relation to the process of citymaking in the platform society.

The set of principles, practices and associated ethics labelled as "hacking" has long been part and parcel of the world of media technologies. We find it amongst the radio-amateurs who in the 1910s and 20s hacked together their own crystal set receivers and discussed both the workings of the technological systems themselves as well as societal issues through the airwaves in a practice they called 'Citizen Radio' (Barlow, 1988). We come across it at the dawn of the 1960s at the labs of the Massachusetts Institute for Technology in Cambridge, where teenagers and undergraduates started tinkering with the newly built giant supercomputer TX-0. Officially designed for defence and research purposes and operated by a closed priest-like class of experts, this expensive machine was now appropriated by the playful explorations of these young outsiders, driven by their curiosity about what such a machine could do. They even designed their own games – upsetting the air of seriousness that had surrounded computers until then.

. . . . . . . .

*Until then, they claimed, computers had mainly been associated with the oppressive workings of a centralized government*

. . . . . . . .

We stumble again upon a hacking ethos in the 1970s, when in the San Francisco Bay Area under the umbrella of the Homebrew Computer Club, a groups of geeks – that later would found tech companies such as Apple - started to build their own computers as an act of political rebellion. Until then, they claimed, computers had mainly been associated with the oppressive workings of a centralized government. Now, they aspired, these same technologies could be used for personal liberation and self-organization, along the line of the hippie era zeitgeist of collaborative self-sufficiency reflected in publications like The Whole Earth Catalogue (Levy, 2001; Turner, 2006). In the 1980s, 'hacking' receives a negative connotation in society at large, when it's associated with criminals who break into computer systems. Films like WarGames (1983), Blade Runner (1982), Tron (1982) and books like Neuromancer (1984) bring this image of the underground semi-criminal hacker into the domain of popular culture, demonstrating the vulnerable aspects of large technological systems. In the 1990s, the hacking community finds itself rehabilitated, as 'hacking' gains broader cultural leverage as a label under which open source programmers have started to collaboratively work on free software such as the Linux kernel, the web browser Mosaic or the online publishing tool Wordpress. Here hacking is interpreted as contributing one's knowledge and mastery over computer systems to the development of software for a common good, while at the same time showing off one's cleverness to do so to a group of peers.

More recently in our current decade, the term hacking has popped up in a similar way to describe a group of people who use computers, digital media and the internet in an effort to shape urban life from the bottom-up. In the introduction of his much-cited book on Smart Cities, Anthony Townsend describes the emergence of the 'civic hacker' as follows:

> "They eschew efficiency, instead seeking to amplify and accelerate the natural sociability of city life. Instead of stockpiling big data, they build mechanisms to share it with others. Instead of optimizing government operations behind the scenes, they create digital interfaces for people to see, touch, and feel the city in completely new ways. Instead of proprietary monopolies, they build collaborative networks. These bottom-up efforts thrive on their small scale but hold the potential to spread virally on the Web. Everywhere that the industry attempts to impose its vision of clean computer centrally managed order, they propose messy decentralized and democratic alternatives." (Townsend, 2013)

Townsend's description is not only the latest instalment of a description of historic hacker cultures, it also brings together many of the characteristics found in the various examples in a neat list of characteristics: hackers are not mere users of technology, but active creators, shapers, and benders of media technologies as well as the relationships mediated through them (see also: Levy, 2001; Roszak, 1986). They like to tinker with technology and cooperate on projects for a common good and prefer messy iterative operations above master plans. Hacking, in other words, refers to the process of clever or playful appropriation of existing technologies or infrastructures, and bending the operation of a particular system beyond its intended purposes or restrictions to serve personal or communal goals.

• • • • • • • •

*Hackers are not mere users of technology, but active creators, shapers, and benders of media technologies*

• • • • • • • •

For hackers, that approach is not just one out of many ways to solve a problem. For many of them it's a way of life. Many of the proponents in the examples given above wilfully make use of the term hacker as a communal badge of identity. To be a hacker not only means to playfully make use of systems beyond their intended logic, it encompasses a complete ethos: a particular way of understanding and operating in society.

It's the combination of these two aspects of hacking that we find interesting vis-à-vis the development of a 21$^{st}$ century collaborative design approach for citymaking. 'Hacking the city' is about finding ways to actively shape one's surroundings through the clever and playful appropriation of technology. And it could also be considered as a communal identity, a collective approach to citymaking that borrows a number of central tenets of the hacker culture. Although it would be naïve to consider the hacker community as a coherent whole, from which we could distil a single, consistent ethic, there are two central themes in the hacker ethic that for us are of particular interest: a culture of sharing and collaboration, and a tinkering, hands-on way to problem-solving.

## HACKERS' STANCE ON INFORMATION: IT WANTS TO BE FREE

The first point is the attitude of hackers towards openness and sharing knowledge. If there's one central principle that runs through various accounts of hacker culture, it is unobstructed access to information (in the form of code) in combination to the freedom to build upon other people's work. 'Information wants to be free' is one of the leading adagios of hacker culture, although there is a controversy about how exactly that should be interpreted. In the 1980s, open software-evangelist Richard Stallman added an important nuance to this claim: 'Think free as in free speech, not free beer.' Free to him did not mean that all information would be accessible without any costs, but that users had the freedom to build upon, alter, change or hack into existing information structures. Such a freedom to information could lead to innovation, and thus contribute to a better world. As such the hacker ethic opposes the closed knowledge systems of patents and proprietary platforms. The more information is available, the better. As Stallman stated:

> "I believe that all generally useful information should be free. By 'free' I am not referring to price, but rather to the freedom to copy the information and to adapt it to one's own uses... When information is generally useful, redistributing it makes humanity wealthier no matter who is distributing and no matter who is receiving." (Stallman, quoted in: Denning, 1996)

The openness of systems has another advantage. In his seminal essay 'The Cathedral and the Bazaar' Eric Raymond (1999), one of the gurus of the open source software movement, explains the decentralized hacker-approach of being small and agile. It's that very ethic of small-scale initiatives in combination with cooperation with one's neighbours that allows the bazaar to respond to needs as they emerge. That is in contrast to the cathedral, which according to Raymond articulates the vision of a master builder, slowly becoming a masterpiece to dominate the urban landscape, yet tied to its original function and unable to adjust to changing circumstances. For Raymond, as for Stallman, not collaborating with peers in developing software was not an option. Now how can new media technologies assist to port this approach of openness, collaborative learning and cooperation from online projects – varying from Wikipedia to open source software – to the process of citymaking? That's one of the leading questions we will try to address in the Hackable City Toolkit further on in this publication.

Hackable City Research Question 2
How can new media technologies assist to port the approaches of openness, collaborative learning and cooperation found in various instances of hacker culture – varying from Wikipedia to open source soft- and hardware – to the process of citymaking?

## HACKERS, EXPERTS AND AMATEURS

The hacker ethic of sharing knowledge opens up another interesting discussion: that of the shifting relation between experts, professionals and citizens. The hacker is an interesting figure: he doesn't belong to a class of officially sanctioned or accredited experts, his knowledge is usually self-taught, and his mode of operation not one of systematic research moving from the formation of strategic plans to application, but rather a more impromptu one of trial and error. As such he may be a figurehead for a broader trend, that according to numerous sociologists consists of a crisis in the 'natural' legitimacy of expert knowledge, systems and professionals, that has started to develop in concurrence with the period of late or high modernity that begins somewhere in the early 1980s (see for example Beck, 1992). This so-called crisis touches many domains - from politics to science to health care to journalism. It also affects urban design, policy making and governance. There is now a continual uncertainty and ongoing need to redefine the role of professional disciplines across the board. There is, then, a need to come up with reflections on and new narratives about the role of the (former) expert in relation to the (professional) amateur (Leadbeater & Miller, 2004).

In professional circles we have seen numerous answers to this trend. In planning we have seen the rise of collaborative planning in which planners have started to use digital tools to gather input from stakeholders or the use of games to engage various stakeholders in the process (Gordon & Manosevitch, 2010; Gordon, Schirra, & Hollander, 2011). In processes of 'open innovation' and 'living labs', procedures have arisen in which citizens can act as co-creators in the design of products or even their neighborhoods. Baccarne et. al. have described these initiatives as evocative of a hacker ethic, as these living labs 'promote the idea that anyone is capable of performing a variety of tasks rather than relying on paid experts or specialists' (Baccarne, Mechant, Schuurma, De Marez, & Colpaert, 2014).

The point is not that expert-knowledge has no value anymore, or that every amateur can take up any task. Rather, what these examples show is that citymaking can be more inclusive if various forms of expertise– from the highly technical to the everyday-life-experiences – can be brought together in a system of open innovation. Or argued the other way around: if the process of city-making is to be made hackable, citizens have to become hackers, meaning that they should have ways to master the knowledge and capacities needed. In a hackable city, urban design is then not just about the design of grand schemes, but also about the design of procedures and tools that can help citizens to contribute to that. This could take various forms, from designing knowledge platforms through which knowledge can be crowdsourced and exchanged, to providing digital tools that can help non-professionals understand or intervene in situations or the organization of capacity building campaigns that help citizens master the skills needed to become active agents of change in the platform society.

A new generation of Dutch architects has already started to embrace this vision. In the book *Reactivate!* Indira van 't Klooster writes how a series of offices have redefined their role. They have designed new procedures of campaigning, crowdsourcing and crowdfunding to approach citizens as co-creators, whereas they have started to see their role as developers or producers of projects that address urgent societal issues, organizing the knowledge and contributions of various stakeholders around it (Van 't Klooster, 2013).

Hackable City Research Question 3
What new procedures of knowledge exchange and capacity building are needed to make the hackable citymaking process an inclusive one?

Hackable City Research Question 4
How can digital media platforms be designed to organize various stakeholders around societal issues and give each stakeholder the opportunity to contribute to the best of their abilities?

## LEARNING BY DOING
Another common trait in various hacker cultures of use to our investigation of city making in the era of the platform society, is hackers' particular approach to innovation: one that consists of a messy learning by doing attitude, based on an attitude of finding intrinsic pleasure in tinkering, balancing pragmatic problem solving and curiosity-driven problem seeking, and considering messiness as a potential strength instead of a threat. A hacker is both a homo faber and a homo ludens, as they tend to have a playful and curious world outlook. They want to know how stuff works by tinkering with it; not as engineers who design according to a carefully preconceived plan or blueprint but in an improvising go-along way. Being a hacker entails a slightly subversive attitude. Hackers do not accept defaults ("as is") but imaginatively enquire the space of potential ("what if"). In an anecdote that illustrates this point, Levy describes the entrance of a fourteen year old boy in the M.I.T lab who started to drive all the theoretical researchers crazy. Where they were used to start building complicated theorems to work from, he just started to play with the computer to see what it could do.

> "They're theorizing all these things and I'm rolling up my sleeves and doing it . . . you find a lot of that in hacking in general. I wasn't approaching it from either a theoretical point of view or an engineering point of view, but from sort of a fun-ness point of view." (Levy, 2001)

In recent years, this learning by doing has increasingly found its way into the process of citymaking. In their book, *Tactical Urbanism,* Mike Lydon and Anthony Garcia describe numerous examples of citizens, designers, architects and even city governments who have just started to try out small and temporary interventions in the urban fabric to see whether they would be successful, rather than commissioning feasibility studies or grand master plans. Whereas playfulness was often used as a tactic to mobilize local stakeholders and potential users, recording metrics about the consequences were often important in convincing stakeholders of a more durable interpretation of the interventions (Lydon & Garcia, 2015).

Hackable City Research Question 5
How can we bring the iterative, learning-by-doing approach to the process of citymaking?

## THE COMMONS: HACKING FOR THE PUBLIC GOOD?

Whereas the notion of a hackable city can bring an interesting perspective to the process of citymaking, it can also be used to problematize this process with digital media. The concept of the hackable city is not a simple remedy that we can apply to our cities. Rather, it's a lens through which we can discuss issues related to the use of digital media in citymaking. Again, the discussions in hacker culture shed some interesting light on this. We want to highlight two such discussions: one centered on the organization of a commons; the second on governance models. The first discussion revolves around the possible conflict between, or alignment of, individual and communal rewards and the production of commons-structured resources. Hacking, as we have seen, revolves around the organization of creativity. As such, it both serves to scratch a very personal itch (I don't like the way something works so I'll modify it according to my wishes) and has a more social side to it (I've come up with something clever and this could benefit others too). This social side is competitive, for many hackers it's about impressing and gaining respect among peers through cleverness (for instance Levy, 2001: 12), and at the same time it involves a communal attitude of openness, sharing-alike and community building (Himanen, 2001; Hippel, 2005; Levy, 2001).

Some have argued that as a mode of production and organizing communities, hacking can be positioned between the capitalist free market economy and communitarian modes of production. In the former, competition and individual profit reign supreme, as well as the associated idea that corporations are the most suited to drive innovation and well-being. The latter departs from ideals of collectivizing and redistributing resources in an equal way. Himanen, for instance, suggests that hacking, as part of a new ethics and spirit of the network society, establishes a third way. Hackers reject the typical capitalist mode of corporate innovation through competition based on controlling information, and at the same time they reject the centralized authority model associated with communism (Himanen, 2001). Himanen's empowered capitalist hacker is not motivated by money but does not reject it, profit is understood in a much more complex system of values comprized of creativity, passion, freedom, social worth, activity, openness and caring.

Although the term is not much used in hacker culture per se, we find it interesting to make a link to the model of the commons – the collective development and management of communal resources, irrespectively of property rights. The commons in medieval feudal England was the land that belonged to a manor but on which the inhabitants of the estate had certain rights, like collecting firewood, hunting or pasture. Later the term was extended to include all resources to which a community has rights upon. These resources could be natural as in the case of pastureland and access to water or technological resources, as for example TV and radio frequencies. Interestingly, the word 'common' derives from the Norman word 'commun', which itself has its roots in the Latin word 'munus', which combines the meanings of "gift" and "duty", stemming from the social obligation of having to return a gift to the person that gave you one. The production of open source software could be seen as an endeavour to develop a communal resource in which various participants contribute their knowledge and time to construct a tool that's available for the community at large. In his Hacker Manifesto, McKenzie Wark explicitly calls for the safeguarding of an information commons, a shared pool of resources free for all to use – and contribute to (Wark, 2004).

Can we think of the process of citymaking in similar terms? Where citymakers work together to create and manage communal resources, not for the sake of individual profit, but from a public interest perspective? This perspective doesn't mean that there shouldn't be a business model or that everyone involved should work for free as in 'free beer'. It means that a business model should serve the public interest rather than being a goal in itself.

•••••••••

*How individuals can be rewarded for their contributions to a common good, is a central question in hackable citymaking practices*

•••••••••

What's of interest for our purposes here, is that there runs a thread through hacker culture that combines the process of open learning with one of collaboration and producing something for the community at large, rather than just for personal profit. At the same time, the hacker ethic is more libertarian (or even anarchistic) than communitarian. There usually is also an individual motivation present to the participation in collaborative projects, usually personal recognition rather than monetary rewards. Although hackers like to share and engage in open innovation, they do also care about individual reputation (Himanen, 2001). Using the analogy of hacking to describe processes of citymaking highlights these tensions between the individual and the collective. How individuals can be rewarded for their contributions to a common good, is a central question in hackable citymaking practices.

Again, we have seen developments in this direction in current practices of citymaking. In his *Compendium for the Civic Economy,* Joost Beunderman provides an overview of numerous initiatives that have started exploring new organization and business models to organize local communities around issues of public interest (Beunderman, 2012). Similarly, the British 'innovation foundation', Nesta, has published a great overview of similar initiatives called Digital Social Innovation. They see a European-wide rise of "collaborative methods for financing, development and production, leading to services that are provided neither by the state nor by the market" (Bria, 2015). Interesting as these examples are, Nesta also sees a challenge here. While local and small scale examples abound, it is still hard to scale these or find room for further experimentation (Bria, 2015).

Hackable City Research Question 6
How can we align, engage and reward various stakeholders around the organization of urban infrastructures or issues as a commons?

## HACKING & GOVERNANCE

A second discussion central to the hacker ethos revolves around the organization model and governance of hackable city processes. As many have pointed out: hackers distrust central authorities and prefer to work in a decentralized way. As Voltaire would say: they mend their own gardens. This leads to two potential challenges: a) the organization and commitment within projects, and b) the relation between a collective project and society at large.

To start with the first issue, some have argued that for the realization of communal goals, the bottom-up approach may be too non-committal. Some advocates of open source software such as Eric Raymond have therefore argued for strong leadership. Successful examples of open source software, he claimed, happened because of the benevolent dictators that oversaw them, the production of the open source browser Netscape being his central exhibit (Raymond, 1999). His argument reflects a wider discussion on the role of centralized positions in horizontal communities. This discussion also directly relates to the necessity of institutions or other central agents that should have an overview and guide processes, even when the processes themselves are open, participatory and hackable. Some projects resolve this internally, but in many projects, new roles may emerge for campaigners, community organizers or civil institutions.

On a second level, conflicts may arise between the goals of a collective practice of hackable city-making, and the public interest at large. The hackable city assumes a form of (civic) empowerment, giving agency to the public to take initiative upon issues of their concern. At the same time, it poses the question of democracy. How do new opportunities for self-organization compare to institutional practices of democratic decision making? In the framework of a hackable city, who secures that the purposes of a self-organised group will not overshadow the interests of the general public? Despite the charm of people joining forces to inflict positive change in their environments, we must not forget that these are also unsolicited actions that may be undemocratic. The discussion on these possible conflicts of interests has recently taken off. On the one hand national and city governments in The Netherlands (and other countries as well) are enthusiastic about the possible rise of a 'participation society' in which it's no longer the welfare state that takes care of all kinds of social provision, but citizens who will organize themselves, start helping out each other. In the 'energetic society' that the Netherlands Environmental Assessment Agency sees emerging, the government is no longer the central director determining both societal goals and the exact path to reach them, but rather a producer that should capitalize on the energy of citizens, organizations, companies and institutions. It should set a framework that various actors then can take up (or 'hack') and fill in according to their preferences and interests (Hajer, 2011). However, Tonkens, Trappenburg, Hurenkamp and Schmidt have recently questioned this approach. This approach may work out fine for the well-educated, but leaves many others who lack the energy, the skills or the willingness to participate in such a way behind (Tonkens, Trappenburg, Hurenkamp & Schmidt, 2015). Similarly, debates have emerged about the legitimacy of citizen-initiatives. To what extent are they representative of the citizenry as a whole? And to what extent are they expressions of private collective interests rather than a public interest? How should local governments relate to these initiatives?

These questions are hard to answer. But again, here the approach of hacking may help finding solutions: rather than designing grand schemes of governance, now is a time for experimenting with various frameworks and models of representation, so we can learn from them.

### Hackable City Research Question 7
What governance frameworks can provide room for citizens and designers to legitimately hack their cities from the perspective of the public interest?

### Hackable City Research Question 8
What new modes of inclusion and exclusion arise in the Hackable City? How can the Hackable City be both inclusive and at the same time provide room for differentiation?

## CITIZENS AND DESIGNERS AS SOCIAL CHANGE AGENTS
To conclude, for us a hackable city is a city that allows citizens or designers to envision themselves as social change agents. That is: they make use of digital tools to appropriate ('hack') one's environment, infrastructure or resources, not so much for personal gain, but rather from the perspective of a common goal or collective interest.

This does not mean that all citizens should become city hackers. Not every citizen has the time, means or interest to become a city hacker. Rather it means that the city as a whole could profit if the system could be opened up to those who see opportunities to hack it from a public interest perspective.

Nor do we claim that planning as a professional discipline will become obsolete. On the contrary, we think there always will be a role for professional designers with their professional knowledge as well as for civil institutions that use democratic procedures to the frameworks for urban development. Rather we seek new ways to organize this process, ways in which citizens, professionals and institutions work together in a process we call citymaking.

We find the notion of the hackable city an interesting lens to discuss the process of citymaking in the era of the platform society. As such the term can be used to highlight critical or contrarian tactics, to point to new collaborative practices amongst citizens mediated through social media, or to describe a changing vision on the relation between governments, designers and citizens. It argues for an iterative approach to citymaking, looking for new ways to share knowledge between and collaborate with a variety of stakeholders. It provides room for both citizens, as well as designers and institutions, to become active agents of change as hackers of their environments.

Whereas the notion of the hacker refers to the means, ethos and practices of individuals to intervene in city making, its companion term hackability refers to the system that is to be hacked, in our case the city. Hacking is often described in terms of a power struggle between hackers and system owners, both in a literal and metaphorical sense. As we argued above, the success of cities as economic and cultural systems depends partially on their hackability. Yet system owners (mainly the government) may or may not set all kinds of legal rules that either facilitate or prohibit the appropriation of urban infrastructures. Can we now imagine an infrastructure of the city (in its broadest sense) that welcomes 'civic hacks'? How could the city as a system be opened up, so hacking into it will be easier for citizens, in such a way that it will still serve the public interest? What could the role of city governments, architects and planners, technologists and citizens be in such an approach? The notion of the hackable city addresses these questions, and at the same time takes a critical stance. It forces us to ask questions about the governance of hackable city projects as well as to identify its risks.

Whereas we have no easy answers to any of the eight questions raised in this framework, we think that finding one or more possible directions to address them is essential to safeguard our cities as democratic and open systems in the era of the platform society. That's what drives our research, and also our first experiments down this road that will be explored further in the Hackable City Toolkit in the next chapter.

# THE HACKABLE CITY TOOLKIT

How can citizens, design professionals, local government institutions and others employ digital media platforms in collaborative processes of urban planning, management and social organization, to contribute to a liveable and resilient city, with a strong social fabric? The goal of our research project is not just to approach this question from a theoretical perspective, but also to explore how new media technologies can be employed in the messy practice of everyday urban life.

In order to answer the latter question, in the period 2013-2014 we carried out a mapping of initiatives in the city of Amsterdam that in some way or another used digital media to 'hack' into the city. That is: we were looking for initiatives that used digital media to organize themselves around particular issues with the goal of improving their direct surroundings or urban life at large. Rather than waiting for policy makers to come up with a solution to a problem, these groups organized themselves to identify issues, organize campaigns around them, and find ways to collaboratively act upon these issues. We also looked at the ways in which projects matched Pekka Himanen's hacker learning model in which a continuously evolving learning and doing environment is shaped by the learners themselves (Himanen, 2001). Another criterion was the presence of a social model that Himanen assigns to the hacker ethic. In this model, projects usually start with somebody's initiative whose limited knowledge or resources only allow him to develop his idea to a certain extent. The project is then opened up to the community to further develop the idea. In all these projects, digital media play a central role as a tool that brings the community together. When these ideas involve projects bound to specific locations, such as community gardens or house construction, the internet is used as an effective means for joining forces and later disseminating and developing the idea further.

We inventoried 84 such projects, varying from groups of people building their own homes, to citizens organizing themselves around local issues such as safety or health, to sharing economy initiatives. Our goal was to try to understand who initiated these projects, what the issues were they are occupied with, and how they tackled them.

·········

*Although many of these projects were initiated by citizens or professionals, many of them operated in cooperation with a variety of institutional stakeholders*

·········

Some of these projects were initiated by citizens, others by professionals. Some rely on voluntary actions, or are financed by state or city subsidies, others were set up as start-ups. Most of them employed both digital technologies as well as offline ways of organization through meet-ups and interventions in public space. They also operated on different scale levels: from the hyper-local to the global.

Through a survey, we identified the stakeholders involved in these projects as well as their goals and uses of digital media. About 70% of the projects that responded to our survey said they were initiated by a newly formed group of individuals, followed by 20% that were initiated by an existing community and 10% were either entrepreneurial or established by non-profit organizations. Many of these projects addressed a personal wish or urge of their initiators. For example Thuisafgehaald.nl was developed as a side project out of the wish of its initiators to share food with their neighbors and try out new homemade dishes. Others are quests for alternative modes of area development initiated by self-employed creatives that look for ways to operate outside traditional schemes. Examples are Glamourmanifest or Cascoland.

Although many of these projects were initiated by citizens or professionals, many of them operated in cooperation with a variety of institutional stakeholders. Many of the projects surveyed reported ties to the 'stadsdelen' (the administrative city government units operating at the level of city districts). The central municipality was also mentioned as stakeholder or partner, but significantly less than the *stadsdelen*, the official term for Amsterdam's City precincts. This shows that many of the projects surveyed are working in a decentralized framework. Of the non-governmental agents, Liander and Ymere stuck out. Liander is the largest utility company in the Netherlands, responsible for the management of the electricity and gas network, mainly in the northern part of the country. It is also a partner in many projects supported by the Amsterdam Economic Board and has initiated a number of energy-related small-scale pilots. Ymere is a housing corporation with a social profile that supports mainly citizen-initiated projects in areas where they manage a large proportion of the buildings.

The issues and goals these projects seek to address can be classified in a three (partially overlapping) main categories:

- A first group of projects seeks to advance a more sustainable management of resources, including themes of energy production and management as well as local food production, urban farming and exchange networks.
- A second group of projects aims to improve social cohesion. Their main objective is to bring people together and encourage them to interact, considering interpersonal interaction something positive on its own. The result is a variety of activities that range from yoga and language lessons to discussion groups, communal gardens and workshops. Neighborhood cultural centres or artistic projects are examples in this area.
- A third group of projects consists of projects that seek to improve the liveability of neighborhoods. These are usually tied to a specific location and aim to upgrade the local conditions. This can be people who gather in order to re-develop their areas, projects that address issues of mobility and access to and the care of the environment.

In our survey, the goal most mentioned was 'More efficient and sustainable resource management'. A large part of these projects deal with the theme of energy. This is either addressed by looking into alternative models of producing energy, e.g. by collectively installing solar panels or windmills or exploring different ways of managing the produced energy, for example by sharing locally produced energy. Many of these projects also try to monitor energy use and test possible applications of smart meters, dynamic pricing etc. on behalf of big energy companies. Many of the urban agriculture and farming projects fit in this category as well, since they also explore new ways to produce food locally.

There are also a large number of projects that have stated as their main goal 'to create or sustain a feeling of community among the inhabitants of a neighborhood' and 'improve social cohesion'. There are many different ways they try to do that, but they are mostly centred around a meeting place and the organization of common activities.

The main difference between these two types of projects lies mainly in who is behind them. Many of the energy projects are initiated or supported by large corporations and are used as pilots for the application of new technologies on a wider scale. In the case of the community building projects, the only large organizations involved are occasionally housing corporations, while the local governments are very often initiating or supporting them.

Seven of the 84 projects we have identified were chosen for an in-depth analysis through interviews and analysis of their media use and practices. These projects were chosen to represent a diverse cross section of the long list of projects, both in terms of theme as well as in organizational structure and the issue of who initiated them. These projects are:

- BSH5, a community of self-builders in Amsterdam North
- Farming the City, a research organization on urban agriculture,
- Join the Pipe, an organization campaigning for tap water drinking,
- Makers+Co, a designers' group empowering a local community,
- Peerby, a sharing economy start-up,
- Ring-Ring, a mobile phone app promoting cycling
- Verbeter de Buurt, a platform for reporting local problems and ideas.

Through the survey and the in-depth analysis, we have constructed a taxonomy of phases we found in the 'hackable citymaking' process as well as a taxonomy of hackable citymaking strategies. We found that hackable citymaking projects go through seven phases, which range from defining the issue to engaging the public around it, providing this public with means to act and ways to institutionalize the city hack. This seven step model is comparable to existing models for social organization or living labs and can be reduced to a single question: How can the public be engaged around a communal issue and act upon it? What is specifically interesting for our research purposes is the role of new media in this process. We found that in many of these phases, they provide new means for the execution of that phase. Although not all projects go through all seven phases or follow the same order in doing so, we found this categorization useful as these seven phases reveal a number of (often implicit) design decisions that influence the ways a hackable city project is organized and hence its effectiveness. These seven phases will be discussed further down.

In addition, in order to be successful, we found that many hackable city projects make use of a variety of strategies. In the projects we studied, we came across eight recurring strategies. These strategies include the organization of knowledge communities to exchange knowledge and enable learning, the setup of trust-building mechanisms and the design of institutional frameworks. Again: not every project makes use of all of these strategies, and the way they do so may vary according to the needs of the project. This list of strategies is also far from exhaustive. Yet we found it insightful to describe eight of these strategies, as they may give organizers and designers of future projects some guidance of the kind of tools and strategies they could revert to. An overview of the strategies we found will be given below in the Hackable City Strategies-section.

In future research, the hackable city phases and hackable city strategies will be developed further. We have started here by singling them out and giving a first array of insights in the role of new media in these phases and strategies. In addition, we have added the description of seven case studies. Whereas our Toolkit (the combination of the Hackable City Phases and the Hackable City Strategies) describes phases and strategies in rather general terms, in the case studies we will describe how they were applied in a number of projects in more detail.

## THE HACKABLE CITY PROCESS

1. Projects start with the definition of an issue by an actor.
2. That issue then has to be communicated. We found that visualization tools play an important part here.
3. Next, a larger public has to be engaged with the issue, through online and offline campaigns.
4. This public needs a platform on which it can be represented in some way or another, and where participants can identify and communicate with others, and learn about the composition of the group.
5. In many cases these platforms serve as a way to ideate upon the issue.
What solutions are thinkable and/or desirable?
6. Once one or more solutions are agreed upon, the public needs means to act upon them, share resources or contribute to the common goal, each according to their means and available resources.
7. Now that a project is up and running, how can it be made to last, and have a sustainable impact on the functioning of the city?

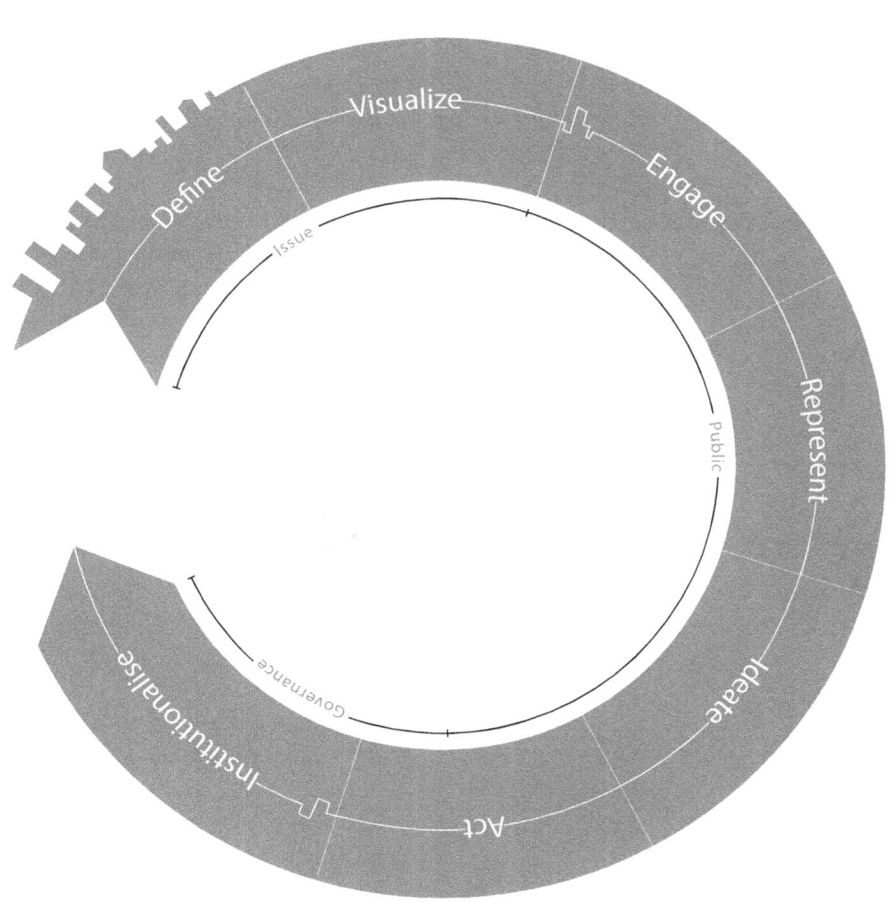

# HACKABLE CITY PHASE 1
## DEFINE AN ISSUE

**Description**  Hackable City projects revolve around a central theme or issue brought up by an initiating actor. An important question is to what extent this process of setting central issues is an open one, or a closed one. Who has the power to come up with issues?

**The role of digital media**  New media can change this step in at least two ways. First, at least theoretically, this process can become more open and democratic, for instance through the use of fora and social media, providing citizens with platforms to voice their concerns. Second, the advent of sensors and the rise of 'big' and open data provide new ways to open up discus sions about societal issues, for instance when citizens start using sensors to monitor air pollution, noise, etc.

KompasopIJburg.nl is a website that offers residents of the Amsterdam neighborhood, Ijburg a tool to name (and vote for) issues they would like to address.

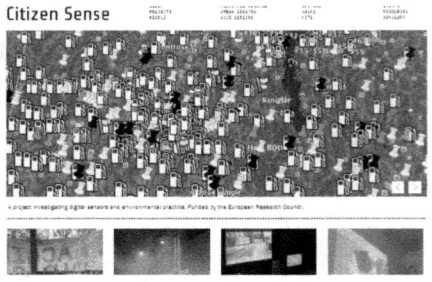

Citizen Sensing or Citizen Science are labels for projects in which citizens have started to gather data about all kinds of societal issues, from noise pollution near airports through sound sensors to collaborative maps that identify how fracking (natural gas extraction) is impacting the living environment.

## HACKABLE CITY PHASE 2
## VISUALIZE AN ISSUE

**Description**  In order to communicate the issue with others, initiators should be able to collect information that can help them build an argument and to visualize this information in ways that engages the public and that can make it operational for the continuation of the initiative.

**The role of digital media**  Datavis allows for new digital ways to visualize issues. This can be done in real time. Another novelty is that digital representation also allows for personalization, so that individual as well as communal concerns and contributions can be visualized.

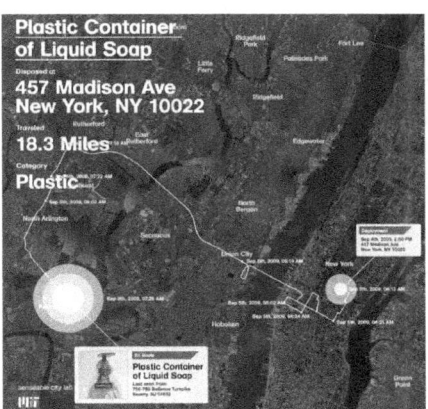

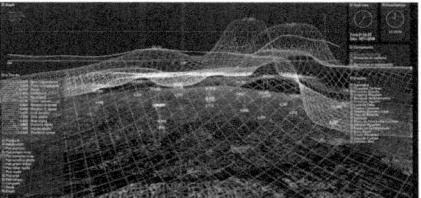

Medialab Prado's project In the Air was one of the first projects that visualized digital data in public space, turning data about air quality in Madrid into a physical 'conversation piece'

MIT's Senseable City's Trash Track project used beautiful maps to make the issue of trash visible in both collective (where does all our trash go), as well as individual (where did my trash end up) ways.

# 3 HACKABLE CITY PHASE
# ENGAGE

**Description**  In this phase, a larger public is to be engaged with the issue. It's about informing potential subjects about the issue and their potential involvement in it, as well as convincing them about its importance. This is not only about showing convincing rational arguments but also addressing the issue at an affective level.

**The role of digital media**  Social media are a new form of campaigning tools, allowing for 'spreadability' of engaging messages. Other new tools in this area are gamification and personalization tools. The former allows for playful opportunities to engage subjects, the latter can show to what extent an issue is affecting individuals, offering opportunities for identification.

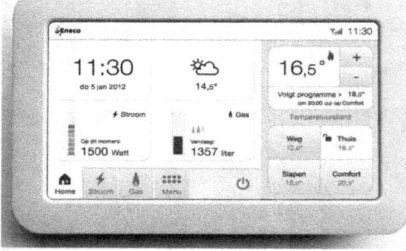

Rezone the Game was a project carried out in Den Bosch that used playful interventions to engage the public with the issue of vacant industrial buildings. It allowed the public to playfully explore the site of a factory, providing them with a new, affective relationship to their environment.

Toon by Eneco is a smart display that publishes real time data about energy use, and allows clients to compare their use to neighbors or friends, providing them with objective information about energy conservation, and at the same time gamifying this goal into a 'comparison game'.

# HACKABLE CITY PHASE 4
## REPRESENT

**Description**  Each public needs to find a way to represent itself, as well as a platform and protocols through which its members can communicate with each other. Strategies range from physical rallies and demonstrations in public space to the use of online discussion for a.

**The role of digital media**  New media provide all kinds of new ways for the representation of publics. The public can be made visible as an aggregate (how much energy have we saved / money have we raised/ bike kilometers have we travelled together), as well as a range of individuals (what are the characteristics / contributions of individual members). Individuals can be represented anonymously, as avatars, through existing social media accounts (e.g. a Facebook ID), with limited information about themselves revealed, or with full profiles. Reputation systems can also help audiences to build up trust.

There is no right or wrong here, just that different publics and different causes ask for different means of representations and means of privacy. Choices in the design of a mode of representation may affect the ways individuals can identify with fellow members of the public, or feel secure within in a community.

In the sharing economy, reputation systems play an important part in the representation of the public, allowing fellow members of the public to evaluate past and potential collaborators. This may help to build up trust and enable individuals to work together on a communal goal. However, it's use has also raised issues about privacy, opportunities to exclude members of different cultural or racial backgrounds as well as the instrumentalization of social relations.

Obscuracam is an app that lets people take pictures of crowds in which the faces of those present are scrambled. This way, the crowd can be represented (look how many of us there are!) without viewers being able to identify individuals within the crowd. Such a tool may come in handy in situations in which the powers that be may not be sympathetic to a crowd of demonstrators.

# HACKABLE CITY PHASE 5
## IDEATE

**Description**  It is important that the public is able to generate ideas and new solutions for the issue at stake. The project itself can function as a platform for dialogue and co-creation.

**The role of digital media**  Digital media can make design tools more accessible through user friendly interfaces that open up the design process to non-professionals. It also provides new tools for (online) deliberation, as well as tools that allow the testing of particular scenarios.

Streetmix is an online tool that allows citizens to design their own streets, by dragging and dropping a number of predesigned categories onto a canvas. Tools like this could help citizens to ideate about redesigns for their neighborhoods, by trying things out and using an easy to understand visual language to communicate their ideas amongst each other.

BaasopZuid is an early example of a playful simulation that allows players to see the consequences of particular policy choices (investing in green spaces vs investing in play grounds) visualized in a neighborhood.

# 6 HACKABLE CITY PHASE ACT

**Description**    In the end, each public needs to find ways to act upon the issue concerned, either as a collective or through individual contributions.

**The role of digital media**    New media offer various new tools for action. First of all, resources can be made available or shared through online platforms, by mapping, sharing or crowdfunding platforms. Second, matchmaking platforms can team up and coordinate individuals willing to act, or distribute large tasks into smaller portions through crowdsourcing. Mapping tools can also turn maps from media of representation into 'action maps': by combining various datasets, locations for interventions in particular domains may become visible.

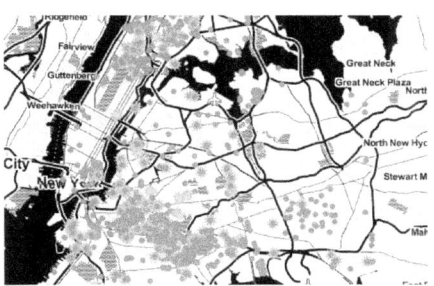

Online collaborative maps such as livinglotsnyc.org give an overview of opportunities to act by mapping empty city lots, providing information about their owners as well as communities that are activating the site.

Crowdfunding and crowdsourcing platforms such as Voorjebuurt.nl allow communities to organize around an event or site in their neighborhood and share resources, both financial as well as non-financial.

# HACKABLE CITY PHASE 7
## INSTITUTIONALIZE

**Description**  How can a hackable city-initiative be made to last? Can they scale-up, be made replicable, or develop ties or spin out to existing institutions?

**The role of digital media**  As this phase is more of about organization and legal and institutional contexts and structures, digital media technologies play less of a role here. Although they could play a role in the way systems interoperate. Through API's or other tools, the data or insights gathered by a hackable city project can be linked to institutional databases or monitoring systems.

Companies such as Airbnb and Uber have grown so much that many municipalities have been forced to consider the implications of these economies for their cities. Recently Airbnb was asked to collect a hotel tax from the listings on the website, formally being recognized as an accomodation provider.

Uber has also consented to share anonimized data about the transportation habits of its clients with city authorities to improve public transportation.

Sometimes established institutions integrate platforms that were developed outside these institutions. For instance, in 2014 Amsterdam Municipality piloted a Dutch version of Change by Us called "Idee voor je Buurt".

# HACKABLE CITY STRATEGIES

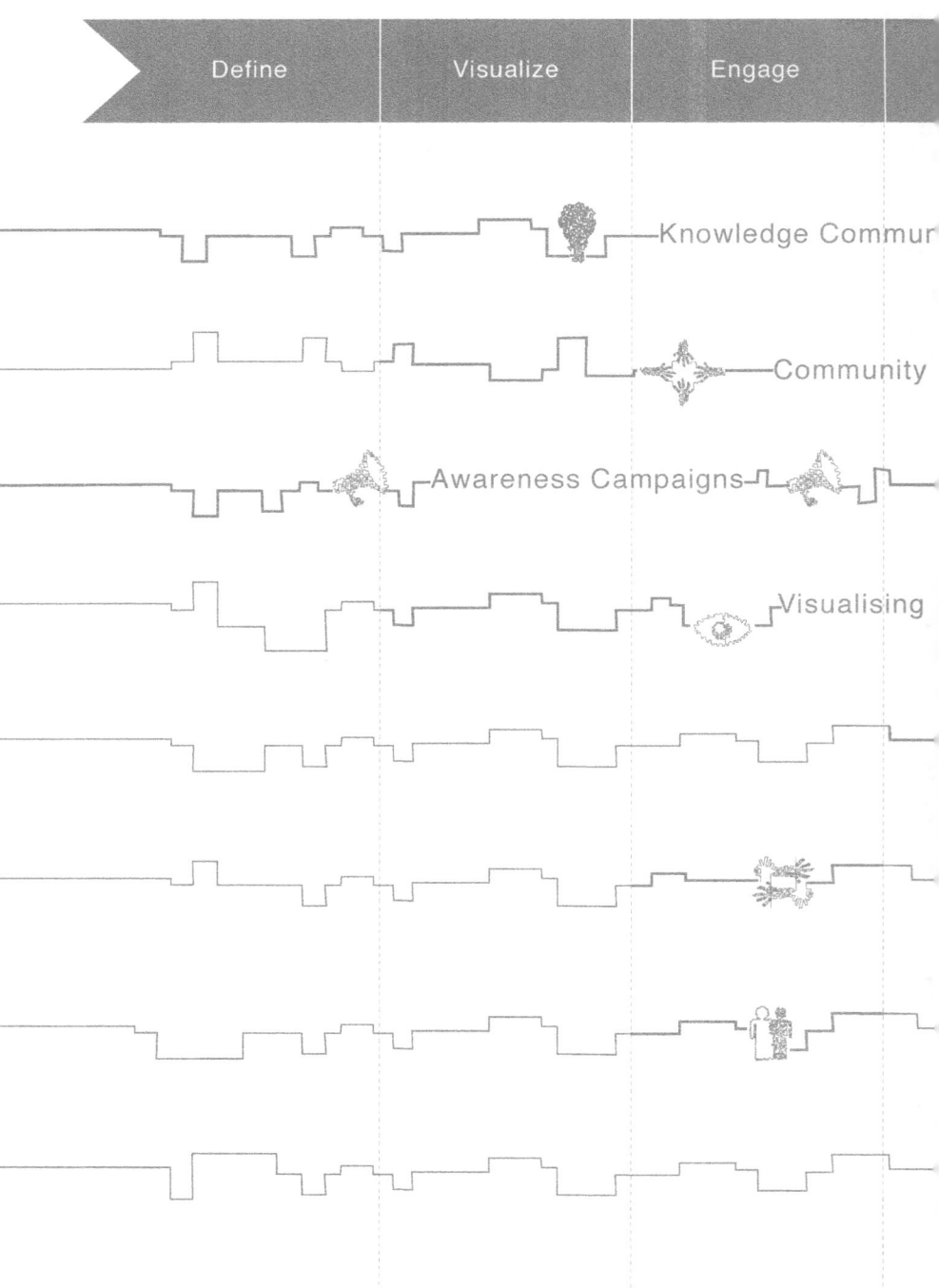

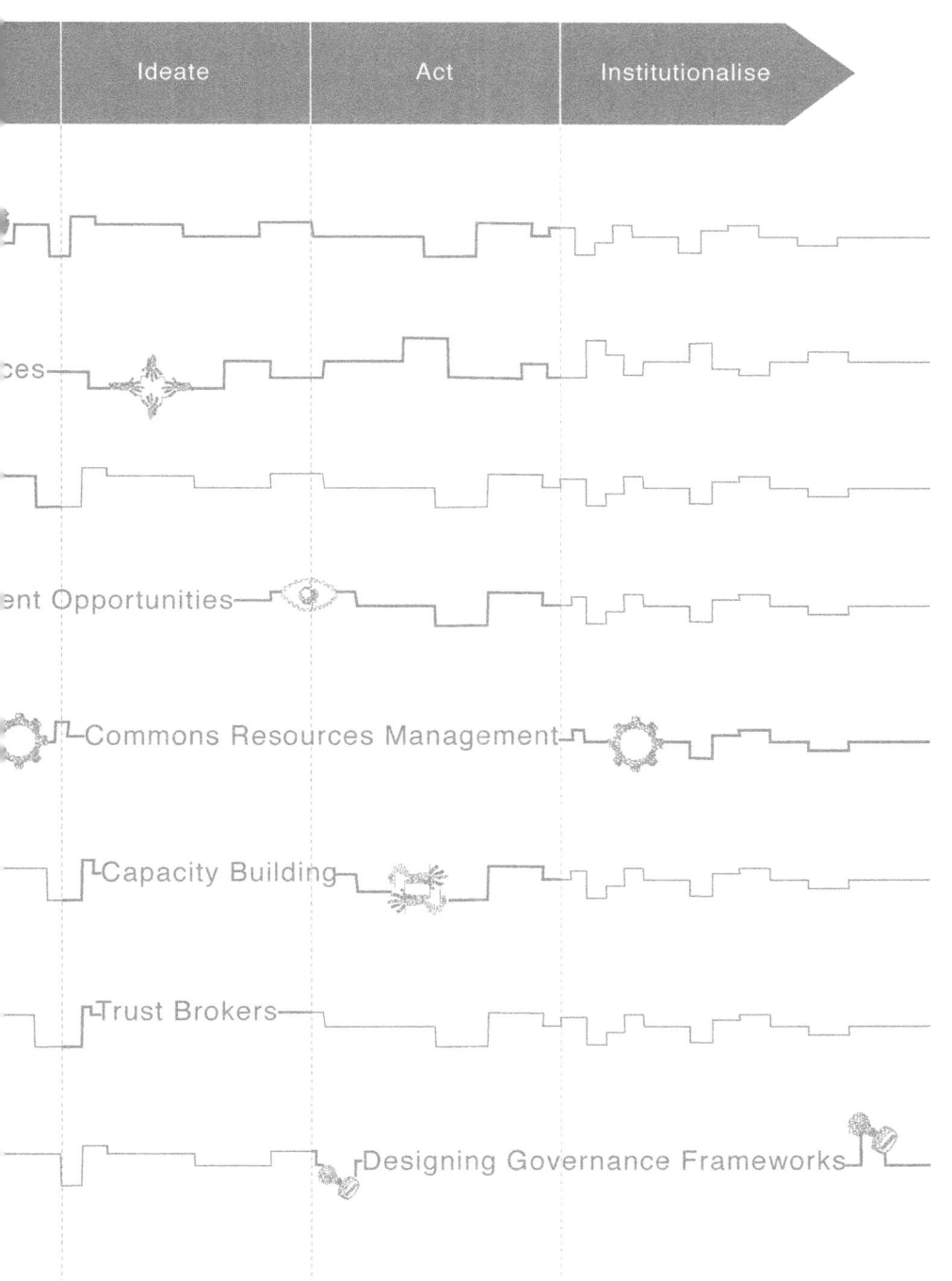

| | Ideate | Act | Institutionalise |
|---|---|---|---|

ces

ent Opportunities

Commons Resources Management

Capacity Building

Trust Brokers

Designing Governance Frameworks

| | |
|---|---|
| Knowledge Communities | A Knowledge Community is a group of people with certain expertise, gained either by education or by intense occupation with a given issue, who are willing to come together and share their knowledge both among themselves and externally. Knowledge Communities are useful to hackable citymaking because they form the first step of creating a pool of collective intelligence and allow participants to learn from each other. It's also a way to institutionalize the knowledge gained in a project and make it available for those who join later. These communities can take the form of physical gatherings, such as a 'knowledge café', or knowledge can be exchanged and codified through mailing lists, forums, social media groups, blogs or wikis. |
| Community Marketplaces | By establishing Community Marketplaces, the members of a group can gain access to products, services, and experiences delivered by their fellow members and exchange them on a peer-to-peer basis. They can take the form of online platforms, social media self-organized groups or mobile phone apps. The exchange of goods and services can be voluntary, or financially rewarded. Sometimes, alternative bookkeeping systems are used (such as time banks). |
| Awareness Campaigns | Awareness Campaigns serve to make an issue visible to a wider public and are usually a first step to engaging a group of people willing to commit time and resources into an issue. It can also serve as a strategy to disseminate the results of an ideation process. Campaigns can have traditional forms of distributing printed material such as posters or flyers, social media campaigns or can take the form of guerrilla interventions and public art projects. Many projects make use of a combination of offline and online campaigns. |
| Capacity Building | Capacity building is an important step for hackable citymaking initiatives because it allows non-expert members of a community to develop their skills, knowledge and abilities, making them feel more empowered to act in the framework of the initiative's engagement, ideation and action steps. Tools that contribute to capacity building include co-creation sessions, workshops, design journeys, storytelling or role-playing. Persuasive or serious games can also play a role here. |

| | |
|---|---|
| Visualizing Development Opportunities | A way to make collected data operational is to present it in a way that it can reveal opportunities for ideation and action. In order to visualize development opportunities, one can employ, among others, tools such as infographics and data visualizations, stakeholder mapping, digital fieldwork and systems maps. The idea is to present (real-time) data analysis in such a way that participants can easily find out where opportunities for action are available. |
| Designing Government Frameworks | Expanding its practices into an institutionalized context and having an influence on a societal scale, a hackable citymaking initiative often needs tools that either improve existing governmental processes or propose alternatives. In order to do that, they need to design new governance frameworks and advocate for their adoption by relevant institutional bodies. In order to achieve that, they might need to write specifications documents and participate in lobbying bodies and organisations. |
| Commons Resources Management | Under this name, we include all tools that regulate the management of existing resources either by proposing new business models around them or by changing the processes with which communities have access to communal resources such as energy. Tools that contribute to Commons Resources Management can be systems that automate the distribution of the particular resource, like smart meters, incentive giving structures like dynamic pricing, or simple scheduling plans among users. |
| Trust Brokers | Under the term Trust Brokers, we include any kind of activity with the goal of increasing the feeling of belonging and connectedness among community members. Many of the projects in our original research stated 'community building' as their primary goal and the tools they used to arrive at that included any kind of low threshold activities, such as collective cooking events, language or dance lessons. Other tools to increase trust among community members can be neighborhood suggestion boxes and informal meetings. |

# CASE STUDIES

### CASE STUDY **BSH5**

BSH5 is an informal group consisting of the self-builders (a Dutch term referring to individuals who are building their own homes, an uncommon practice in the Netherlands due to regulation) of 18 small plots on a collective lot ('Lot 5') in Buiksloterham, a brownfield redevelopment in the northern part of Amsterdam. Since 2011, BSH5 is organized via personal meetings, a website and a mailing list that allows the group members to coordinate their activities and exchange experience. Their objective is not only to develop their individual houses, but also to contribute design suggestions for the neighbouring public space, a community centre, a shared warehouse, as well as to create temporary urban gardens in empty pieces of land and to create a 'dream atlas', a repository of ideas about Buiksloterham.

The Municipality of Amsterdam decided to allocate several plots of land in the former industrial area of Buiksloterham for development by individual users on the basis of a 50-year lease. Early adopters of this development model, such as those in Lot 5, were mostly architects and designers. Their professional occupation allowed them to appreciate the opportunity and estimate the necessary time and costs involved. The initial success of Lot5 led to the allocation of several other lots of varied sizes, with a higher diversity of involved self-developers. In 2013, it was estimated that about 210 houses and apartments would be self-build in the Buiksloterham area. According to Martijn Meester, owner of one of the plots in Lot5, getting together to form a group emerged out of necessity. All future inhabitants were encouraged by the Municipality to come together and figure out how they could profit from their collaboration. Their collaboration was partly meant to coordinate major building activities and practical things, such as laying the foundations and negotiating better prices for building materials with retailers. Resources concerning sustainable building solutions, energy provision, materials and even the designs of the houses are collected in the BSH5 website, which also hosts a blog with news about the building process. Evidently, this community was not formed out of an ideal about 'knowing your neighbours' but out of self-interested individuals engaged in a common activity. At the same time, social benefits emerged as a side product; as people got to know each other, a community of neighbours formed even before people actually moved into their new houses. The contact with the Municipality has been very smooth and helpful for the inhabitants. Since it is the first time the city has made such an effort, it was a learning-by-doing process for all the involved parties. Especially in the beginning when the contracts were set up, the Municipality was very open to suggestions on how to make this happen and sought to understand what their actions might mean for the future development of this place.

This positive feedback loop between the city and the self-builders continued after the completion of the houses with the residents having an active voice in issues that affect the public space in the vicinity of their properties. In May 2013, the inhabitants of Lot 5 submitted their proposal for the design of the Bosrankstraat, which the City accepted as a starting point for the technical development into a final design. But this close relationship between the Municipality and the self-builders is also criticized. According to the local neighborhood blog 'I love Noord', the self-builders are trying to create a gated community under the guise of child-friendliness and greener surroundings.
www.ilovenoord.nl/2014/07/gated-community-in-buiksloterham/#sthash.womF934z.gbpl

## RUNNING A BLOG AS A KNOWLEDGE COMMUNITY

BSH5 is a hackable citymaking case in that it brings together two parties that have not traditionally collaborated in urban development. The Amsterdam Municipality circumvented housing corporations and big developers and addressed individuals interested in developing their houses. This created a knowledge community of people with a common goal and their collective experience fed into a policy change from the side of the City, setting the basis for the design of a new governance framework.

At its current state, BSH5 is a group of 30-40 people, living in 15 households spread over 18 plots. The small size of the community was a reason to maintain an informal structure and not organize into a foundation or any other legal form. BSH5 is not a community primarily driven by ICT. They rely on their interpersonal relations and make very little use of digital tools. They use a mailing list to organize internally and a Wordpress-based website where each one can post under their own name either updates on the construction of their houses or solutions and ideas on particular construction issues. There is also a closed Facebook group, called 'Individuele zelfbouw in Buiksloterham' with 37 members, including self-builders and other local entrepreneurs. The discussion concerns news about Amsterdam Noord and the development of the buildings. The digital media they use influences neither the ideation nor the direct actions that stem from their collaboration.

As a community, BSH5 is mostly concerned with very practical issues that concern the construction of their homes. With most of them being architects themselves, BSH5 is a knowledge community that directly puts their expertise to work for this small-scale development project. They exchange solutions on how to do things in a house, such as dealing with energy, internet, heating and so on and they share their research on costs and how long things take. Collectively, they have undertaken more complex tasks, such as laying the foundation, but they have also negotiated with retailers for better prices by ordering large amounts of material.

At the beginning of this process, the people involved had a lot of meetings and aspired to make a book and a film about their experiment, an ambition that became a second priority as the practicalities of building construction slowly took over. The online knowledge exchange and coordination meetings and constant exchange of e-mails gave way to face-to-face contact, now that the building site is the regular meeting place. As a group, they don't actively try to spread their experience. They share ideas on the website and they still hope to make the film at some point, but BSH5 is a rather closed community, with not much interest in externalising its experience. All in all, they consider the city's initiative successful and hope that this way of development will become a formal process within the city of Amsterdam.

From the side of the Municipality, the same experiment has been repeated in 6 other lots, which were proposed for self-development, showing the intention to institutionalize this process and adjust the legal framework so that it can be applied in other areas and create a new model of urban development.

From a Hackable City perspective, this example raises a number of issues. What is interesting is that this approach of area development through self-builders provides citizens with more opportunities to have a say in the development process of the city, both for their individual homes as well as for the design of collective resources such as parks and urban infrastructures. Opening up the development of the city for these parties could lead to more innovative and sustainable approaches.

A knowledge exchange has been set up that allows participants to learn from each other, and at the same time allows government institutions to learn about the process as well. Feedback from the experiences of the self-builders is fed back into the instigation of new development frameworks for the next self-building site. The question that remains is how this process can be made more durable. Knowledge exchange occurs mostly through informal networks within the community itself, with limited opportunity for newly found self-building groups to tap into the knowledge base. Similarly, a need may emerge to also make the assessment of the self-builders actions by the government more lasting. How can their experiences and contributions (or lack thereof) in relation to the public interest (e.g. their involvement in public space development, innovative ways of building environmentally sustainable homes) be measured or otherwise indicated? And how can the outcomes of these processes be fed back into new tender procedures or development frameworks?

## CASE STUDY **FARMING THE CITY**

Farming the City is a research project and online platform investigating the impact of local food initiatives and urban agriculture in built environments, economic systems and community cohesion in the global north. In November 2010, Farming the City started by launching an online platform to collect urban agriculture projects, plots of land available to potential urban farmers and volunteers who wished to support this type of project. This online tool was intended to stimulate a global knowledge community and lead to replicable projects in many cities in the global north. Since August 2013, Farming the City' s team became an independent business and policy advisory group for the development of innovative food-related initiatives.

Farming the City started out with the ambition to use urban farming to reactivate derelict urban areas, but this proved to be very ambitious and rather naïve, as they soon realized that the food process is much more complex and changes are needed in the whole production cycle. But even though it is impossible to be completely self-sufficient by cultivating one's own food in an urban setting , there are many social benefits from engaging in urban agriculture. Farming the City mapped Amsterdam's urban agriculture scene, depicting its characteristics and connecting its stakeholders, and adopted the food production and distribution system, as the main framework within which to position several case studies.

Their first research findings revealed that there are people with very different backgrounds and identities that share the goal of reconnecting the production and consumption of food in urban environments, but despite the fact that they all work in the same field they rarely interact with each other. With the support of Amsterdam Municipality, they consequently put together a map of Amsterdam with 19 innovative case studies, organized per Stadsdeel (city district), realizing that most projects address mostly sourcing and consuming food and not packaging or transportation. In order to test these observations on a larger scale, they launched an online application with the same goal, which functioned as a database of projects, people and ideas on a global scale. This fulfilled a double goal of the organization: on one hand to focus on Amsterdam and map the people who are involved in local food processes (sourcing, preparation, transportation and consumption), look at how they participate, what their needs and problems are, and on the other hand to use a global input for inspiration, while expanding the community of landowners, food growers and volunteers.

## VISUALIZING DEVELOPMENT OPPORTUNITIES THROUGH ONLINE MAPS

The online platform collected different types of information depending on the project, such as location, type (roof, garden, plot etc.), how many paid people were working there, how many volunteers and the scale of the project by means of a questionnaire. This information was then formatted into reports meant to share knowledge among experienced and prospective urban farmers. Additionally, landowners could indicate the position and size of their empty plots and offer them for cultivation. In response, people could volunteer to cultivate or to participate in an existing project. Others could propose a project they would like to start and ask for a piece of land to host their ideas. However, they did not actively map and support the interaction among community members and the resources they collected were inspiring but hardly helpful for their hands-on projects in Amsterdam.

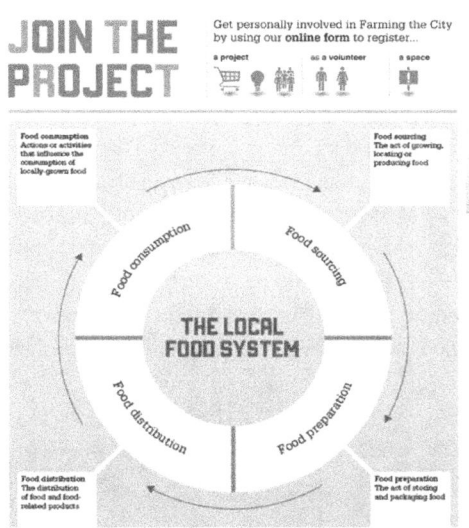

The platform stayed online until 2013 and it was growing in terms of active users and projects mentioned but eventually, Farming the City deemed the global input difficult to manage and often unable to directly contribute to their local projects and decided to take the platform offline in order to focus on the actual projects and people in Amsterdam. Digital media had been useful for communication but in terms of producing content, face-to-face meetings and testing things in reality are irreplaceable. The online platform created an inspiring database of projects, ideas and technical solutions from all over the world, but these projects were often too site-specific to be directly applicable in Amsterdam and the community was too loose to actually profit from their interaction.

At the same time, the local community in Amsterdam was able to meet face-to-face in order to exchange practical ideas and experiences. As a result, Farming the City actually decided to downsize their reach and focus on the city scale, adjusting their plans for a similar app that would function in the same way as the online platform but within Amsterdam, so that people could find projects and gardens where they could farm. Farming the City still maintains an active online presence but it is mostly to report on their activities, rather than a two-way communication.

Farming the City's online platform aimed to fulfil a double function as a Knowledge Community of people with some experience or interest in urban agriculture who would share their practical understanding of food production and as a Community Marketplace where urban farming projects could find volunteers willing to invest their time and knowledge to support them and land owners who could offer their land to be cultivated. At the same time, it aimed to become a tool for Visualizing Development Opportunities, leading to a new business model of sustainable food transportation, and to create a practical guide of getting an urban farming project off the ground in the city of Amsterdam.

## CASE STUDY **JOIN THE PIPE**

Join the Pipe is a small organization that aims to redefine the drinking water distribution system, by campaigning against bottled water and promoting drinking tap water. Join the Pipe was driven by the observation that although in the Netherlands tap water is of very high quality, bottled water sales are rising, because of people's preference to convenience. But bottled water is both a lot more expensive and generates a large amount of plastic garbage. In order to change the habit of consuming bottled water, Join the Pipe provides easy access to tap water in public spaces by installing public water taps. Additionally, Join the Pipe sells design water bottles to individuals and water carafes to restaurants and allocates its profits to water-related projects in the developing world.

In the terms of hackable citymaking: Join the Pipe is hacking into the existing water distribution and consumption infrastructure, in order to create a new cultural practice with a positive impact on the environment and side effects beneficial for the developing world. It is doing that by proposing alternative business models for the management of drinkable water and using diverse campaign tactics for promoting its goal.

The main idea of Join the Pipe is to create a mutually beneficial condition for the Netherlands and for several communities in the developing world, by eliminating plastic garbage in the first case and by providing clean, drinkable water in the second. Their campaigning includes a variety of tools. Apart from the physical presence of the water taps in public spaces, Join the Pipe pays a lot of attention to the media coverage of the placement of the water taps, thus proposing a cultural change around water consumption, and installs temporary taps during public events.

## TURNING DRINKING WATER INTO A COMMONS

Join the Pipe was started in 2008 by a small group of people, contacting Municipalities, railway stations, sports clubs and schools, asking them if Join the Pipe could place water stations in their premises or in other areas with public access. The money earned from these projects would be allocated to fund water stations in African communities. Currently, there are about 350 taps in public spaces around the country; a number that is gradually increasing and allows the company to make plans to expand in Germany. Concerning other countries, the process of setting up branches is very slow and expensive and mostly depends on the amount of actual or potential projects. The nature of their work, which includes various campaigning tools that are connected to a specific site, makes it difficult to expand without strong local connections, which take time to develop.

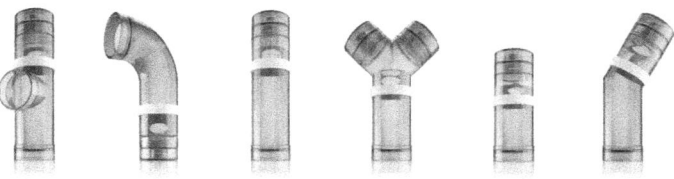

The main issues that Join the Pipe tries to address in the Netherlands are the increased amount of plastic waste, inaccessible tap water, and the increased consumption of sweet beverages in place of water. The organization generally engages in more traditional marketing campaigns, such as partnering with festivals that donate part of their earnings for water projects or with an amusement park that includes the initiative in their advertising. They participate at events and fairs about water sanitation and sustainability, which is their main source of clients. Finally, significant attention is placed in promoting the design bottles. The funny shaped bottles attract attention and are a mobile advertisement for the projects.

## AWARENESS CAMPAIGNS THROUGH SOCIAL MEDIA

Join the Pipe is primarily a campaigning organization so the use of social media is a big part of their strategy with regular posts on both Facebook and Twitter. Its campaigns are mainly about spreading the word and do not explicitly aim to connect the people interested with each other. The content on the website is updated regularly and concerns mostly the promotion of the organization's activities, events, accomplishments and partners. There is no external content or references to other projects or resources about water management. The website mentions a community of 3500 people (25.000 in the Dutch version). However, these people are neither visible on the website nor do they have any way of knowing and communicating with each other. Other ways to inform the public are through restaurants that serve tap water and explain the story on each table and of course, through the bottles themselves, that also have the Join the Pipe message written on the bottom. Especially in Africa, where internet use is not common, they try to approach local radio stations and work with word of mouth.

## CASE STUDY **MAKERS + CO**

Makers+co is a group of designers that connect crafts with social innovation in Amsterdam's Nieuw West area. Their goal is to act as Trust Brokers among the local inhabitants providing low threshold activities that can create a feeling of community and connectedness among the residents of the area. Together with other designers and creators, they focus explicitly on people who want to discover their talents, develop their skills and enjoy the feeling of creating something new. Makers+co organizes (local) partnerships and embeds them in long-term trajectories. Together with their partners, they work towards a platform for 'new creators' by means of the Makers Lab, a workplace for media and crafts in their home location, Garage Notweg, a co-working space in Nieuw West.

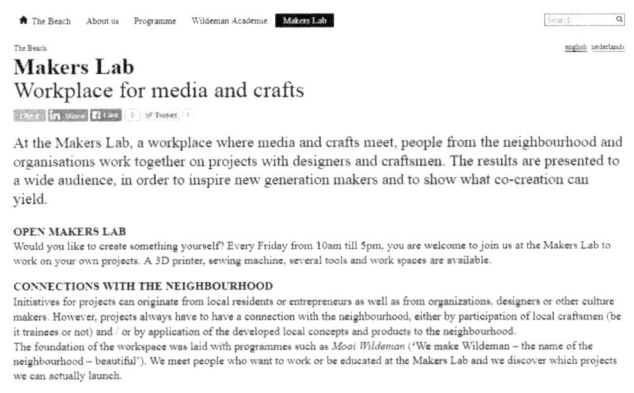

Makers+co was initiated by The Beach Foundation and is the product of several designers' preoccupation about the changing role of the designer and what they perceive as a shift towards co-creation. In their effort to collaborate with non-designers, they realized that they had to lower the threshold and make the design-to-product process more accessible. Their activities assist capacity building mainly for the youngsters and the women of the area. They include workshops with new technologies such as smart textiles, 3D printing and music instrument hacks. Makers+co was launched with a festival, which served as an introduction both to the neighborhood and the local design world. They started off by offering workshops targeted to local women and children, but they soon discovered that offering programs is different from engaging potential participants in actively proposing the types of activities that they want to do. Every Tuesday they held an open café, discussed with people who came with ideas and did some creative sessions to map out the skills present in the area. Out of these meetings a community started forming as well as the first activities, which included, among others, collective cooking and bread baking sessions, a communal garden, and a wooden playground.

At the beginning of Makers + Co, the initiators wanted to address people from the whole Nieuw West, which is an area home to 140.000 people, but soon realized that this scope could not result in the development of meaningful relationships with specific neighborhoods and their people. Depending on the project, they work with a network approach with several other local organisations, each one strongly related to their areas. Their activities are organized around three pillars: 1. community building, which means developing skills, bringing people together and connecting to the creative community of Amsterdam, 2. develop a method for design and making, the Maker Lab, where people can practically experiment and learn, and 3. stage events where people can present their work to the public, invite their friends and family and feel proud of what they have achieved and stay motivated to continue. Makers+co keep a distance from the municipal agenda so they can be autonomous in their choices and create their programs together with the people who are involved in their meetings. They see themselves as activists even though they do not profile themselves as such, but as partners of the people in the neighborhood, who wish to put their ideas forward. They have observed a mistrust and disappointment towards official institutions and don't want to be associated with them; their independence is a way to maintain people's trust.

Makers+co's most prominent goal is to reverse what they perceive as people constantly complaining about safety, playgrounds, bad housing, local government, housing corporations, their neighbours, and turn all this into a proactive mindset. Directly addressing the inequality of skills and education, particularly in the peripheral neighborhoods of the city, by creating an institutionalized framework where people can connect to each other, develop their skills and feel included in the local community, Makers+co act as Capacity Builders and Trust Brokers for Nieuw West.

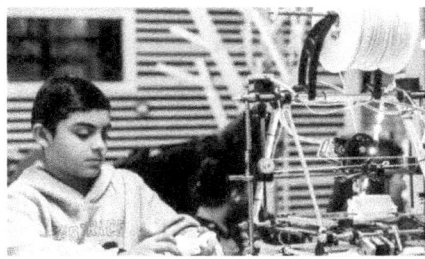 

## TRUST BROKERING AND CAPACITY BUILDING THROUGH EVENTS

An important aspect of their work is to bring new technologies closer to non-professionals. In many of their activities, they have collaborated with Amsterdam-based eculture organizations such as Mediamatic, the Waag Society and Steim to produce workshops where participants could learn about and prototype using 3D design software and printing, sensors and arduino kits.

This comes to a sharp contrast with the limited use of online media. Makers+Co doesn't have an independent website and their social media networks are rather limited in reach. Content wise they work as a depository of images and reports about their activities, and are not regularly updated. Despite their limited reach, social media play a very important role in their communication. Every workshop is announced and documented online and many people use social media to share what they did because they are proud of it. In this way the results of each activity get spread and Makers+co use this as an indicator of success for their events. People don't feel exposed and they even feel comfortable with showing children online, an aspect that project initiator Diana Krabbendam found surprising. The organization's website "Nieuw West Express" (http://www.nieuwwestexpress.nl/) collects a thorough documentation of all the workshops and the results that come out of them. Other common means are flyers, even translated into Arabic by a volunteer from the neighborhood and, of course, word of mouth.

The most successful way to invite people to join however is to invite them personally, so Makers+co calls or sends personal e-mails and try to approach them via the "ambassadors" of the neighborhood. The primary school in the neighborhood is also an entrance to a lot of families. When it comes to dealing with institutionalization, Makers+co don't actively lobby to change things but they have an informal advisory role, as they regularly talk with the local representatives and explain how things are going in the area and how they think about improvements. Working in such a small scale becomes a lot simpler by the fact that people simply know each other personally, so it is relatively easy to approach each other. There is a regular collaboration, both with the city as with other local institutions (eg. housing corporations) and as these parties very often fund Makers+co activities, they care to find more ways to work together. On the other hand, many times Makers+co take initiatives and go ahead with them, considering that this is a way to work faster and manage expectations better.

## CASE STUDY **PEERBY**

Peerby is an online platform and mobile phone app that allows people to borrow things they need from others in their vicinity. It is a Community Marketplace where users can make better use of their collective resources by sharing them within a bigger group. According to the developers, people do not have to buy things they only need to use once in a while, which saves them money, they make better use of collective resources and they are encouraged to get in contact with new people in their neighborhoods. Sharing things means that fewer products need to be produced and thus it allows people to live more ecologically sustainable lives. Additionally, many times the exchange not only revolves about the item itself, but also leads to conversations on how one should use it, the exchange of tips or even to neighbours helping each other out.

What Peerby considers as their strongest point is that their app is question-based, which means that users ask directly for the item they want to borrow, instead of looking through lists of available items. Their query is sent by e-mail to the closest 100 active users within cycle distance. People who get this notification can respond with a 'yes', 'no' or 'not now'. If they respond positively, then they are connected to arrange an appointment. Peerby manages to provide a response to 80% of the questions it receives, within less than 30 minutes. In a nutshell, Peerby tries to match demand and offer within a specific area, promoting access over ownership. Peerby's custom made platform is its basic tool of operation, as the company's action stops when two users get in contact with each other. Other than the platform itself, community management is central to Peerby, with daily updates on their social media accounts.

At the moment, Peerby is active in the Netherlands and Belgium and is looking into a 'scalable growth' model for other countries, via an 'ambassadors' program. Anybody in a new location can take the initiative to become an 'ambassador', collect 100 people who want to join and contact Peerby to 'unlock' this area and be sure that there will enough users to make it work.

Their conviction that the future will be based on a circular economy urges Peerby to experiment with two types of potential business models. In the short term, they are looking into offering insurance for high-value items and premium subscription models but in the long term they are talking with producers to provide community-owned products. These products will be collectively owned by a group of people; when demand increases for one object, a second one can be acquired and so on. The producer will also receive back and recycle worn out or broken items to close the loop.

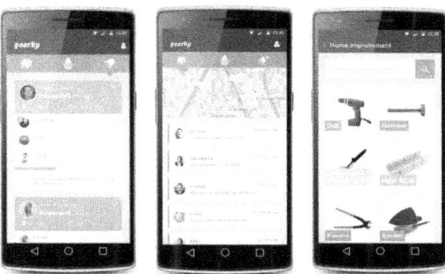

## COMMONS RESOURCES MANAGEMENT
The main issues Peerby tries to address are the economic and resource crisis, to explore new ways of community forming and experiment with technological possibilities. What makes this project an example of hackable citymaking is the fact that Peerby proposes an alternative model of managing resources, as a collectively administered commons, accessed when in need instead of owned.

When Peerby first started, they took a very active approach to convince enough people per neighborhood to join in order to ensure a base of participants dense enough to allow the idea to function. They targeted specific neighborhoods and tried to connect with existing local networks. In this way they ran one-month long neighborhood campaigns which concluded with a big party, publicly rewarding the people who managed to recruit more followers.

From then on, they have worked predominantly through word of mouth and social media. The indirect, free publicity they received because of the positive press reviews were also important.

According to communications manager Ieteke Schouten, this is because Peerby sees the management of stuff in an area as a logistic problem, which can potentially cover the needs of all the inhabitants while at the same time it follows an existing trend of more local community forming, where people look for ways to reconnect with their neighbours.

In terms of representation, however, the app users have no overview of the other platform users and can only contact a small number of them when one poses a question. Thus, the public at any given moment is never larger than 100 people and has no means to understand themselves as a body of like-minded people.

In terms of working together with the city, Peerby initially thought the municipality could be a portal to individual neighborhoods, but their early approaches fell on deaf ears. Now that the project has had a positive course and more sharing economy initiatives are sprouting, they recognize more openness on the part of the city. However, Peerby is developing very fast and growing increasingly concerned with the lack of regulation around sharing economies. That's why they have joined forces with other similar initiatives to advocate for a change in the legal framework regarding sharing economies through the creation of ShareNL, a joint initiative by Peerby, Konnektid, Toogethr, Snappcar, Thuisafgehaald and FLOOW2, that deals with issues of the sharing economy in the Netherlands and engages in dialogue with legislators for the establishment of new regulations that can support these new types of activities. The main issues they address with regards to governance concern control and taxation of sharing economy activities, worker's rights and insurance of involved parties.

## CASE STUDY **RING RING**

Ring-Ring is a citizen-initiated pilot project that campaigns for more extensive use of the bicycle by rewarding cycling kilometres. Ring-Ring targets the IJburg local community in a playful way by gamifying cycling via a mobile phone app. There are personal rewards, for example, discounts in local shops and a quarterly winner for having cycled the most. Other rewards have a collective character. For instance, for every kilometre biked, a small amount of money is allocated to neighborhood funds by the city government. At the same time Ring-Ring is actively lobbying for the change of the legal framework so that cyclists are rewarded for their healthy and environmentally friendly choice with tax-exemptions.

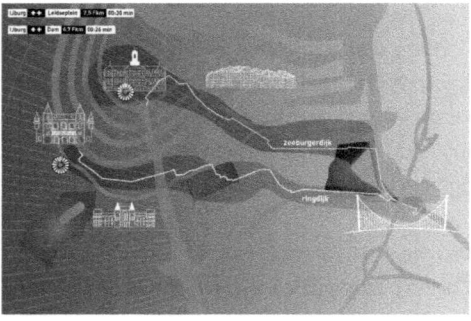
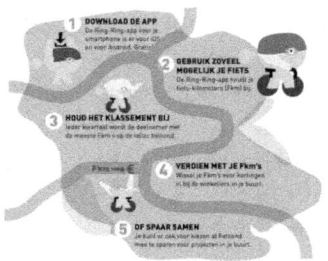

Ring-Ring is the personal initiative of Janine Hogendoorn, who found herself in a position of having to commute a long distance from her new house in IJburg to her work in the city centre. After trying all different modes of transport, she decided that the 30 minute long cycle ride was not as difficult as she originally thought and embarked on an effort to convince others to do the same. She noticed that many people complain about rising health care costs, child obesity and other negative effects of a sedentary life while, at the same time, cycling, which is so widespread in the Netherlands, is framed negatively, with a lot of attention to accidents, lack of bike racks, and insufficient infrastructure. According to Hogendoorn, employers compensate traveling costs when one commutes by car, for example, but there is no reward for using the bike, which is both environmentally friendlier and healthier for its user. After initial plans to open an information shop about cycling, she started looking for other people who might be interested in join forces with her, managed to get the government to look at her research about the benefits of cycling, got a European subsidy and went on to create Ring-Ring as a research-by-doing test.

The underlying concept is that choosing the healthiest and fastest way of urban commuting should be rewarded based on usage. This can be measured via one's smartphone, which is much cheaper than any custom made gadget. The phone knows the owner's departure time, acceleration and route and based on these can be 90% sure that one is cycling.

Even though Hogendoorn, defines herself as an activist, she finds it important that people can join Ring-Ring for their own reasons, so she is purposely trying to avoid giving a specific identity to the app. Cycling can fit into many types of agendas, be it about public space, health, traffic management, air quality and so on, so she doesn't want to exclude any potential users. Ring-Ring's main effort is to make people proud of cycling and there are no better ambassadors than cyclists themselves.

## AWARENESS CAMPAIGNS

Apart from the iPhone and Android mobile phone app, which is the central enabler of engagement and action, Hogendoorm collects all her research and resources around the benefits of cycling at the Ring-Ring website in a blog format. She uses a Facebook and Twitter page to communicate updates about the development of Ring-Ring, which is still in beta, and to advocate for more extended use of bicycles, by presenting news items related to cycling regulation and best practices from other countries.

Hogendoorn aims that her project will become a standard in the Netherlands and aims to reach about 10% of all cyclists in the country. At the moment, about 24% of all people cycle to work, making this an ambitious goal to reach. She is also looking at how Ring-Ring could expand and remain local at the same time. For example, collective miles could be distributed according to the user's postal code and local shops could use this information to join as well. A larger diversity of investors would also significantly improve the project and provide credibility and health insurance companies could join in.

With the main issue addressed by Ring-Ring being to get people out of their cars and on their bikes, the data collected by the app can show where people cycle the most and when. These insights can be used to make these routes faster and safer. Ring-Ring could also be used to visualize the issue simply by exposing the amount of cycle miles and the routes people prefer. So Ring-Ring functions primarily as an awareness campaigning tool for hackable citymaking.
In its efforts to affect legislation it is also advocating for a different way to look at mobility infrastructure in connection to health and environment and acts both as a tool for commons resource management and designing new governance frameworks. The use of the app is anonymous, so there is no communication between the programmers and the users, which prevents Ring-Ring from getting feedback from its users. Other information that finds its way into this project, mostly for promotional purposes, comes mainly from theoretical research into the benefits of cycling. According to Hogendoorn, Ring Ring doesn't use any open data available but generates its own. She has approached the government in order to make use of the data they collect to complement their databases. They feel that, in this way, they can contribute to the improvement of cyclists' infrastructure. In order to promote Ring-Ring, its initiator uses social media and works a lot with local newspapers and the local community website. She has also actively tried to promote the project on bigger scale organizations, such as TEDx and the Major's Challenge, but for the app promotion, face to face daily communication with other IJburgers remains the most convincing practice.

She admits that people feel overwhelmed by the information they receive and the things that require their attention, so the repetition of the message in as many media as she can manage is key to her communication tactics. According to Hogendoorn, people really enjoy the playful approach of the app. One of the main ways of engaging the app's public is the collective cycling kilometres. In this case the goal is always very precise and people are motivated to participate. At the time of the interview, cyclists were gathering points and funds for a WW2 monument, and the next collective project was going to be an education project in the neighborhood park about animals.

## CASE STUDY **VERBETER DE BUURT**
Verbeterdebuurt is an online platform and mobile phone app that makes reporting in the public space more transparent and easy. It allows citizens to monitor local conditions in their neighborhood, report problems and propose ideas, which are forwarded to the local governments. This is done by providing the reporter with more information about the progress of their report, as well as the opportunity to rate the handling of the report by the local council.

Reporting a problem in the local municipality can be quite a hassle. Most districts provide only an e-mail or a phone number with the process itself being quite complicated, so the design office Creative Crowds thought there was room for improvement. Verbeter de Buurt started as a simple Google Maps overlay and soon evolved into an app. Despite initial resistance from city

 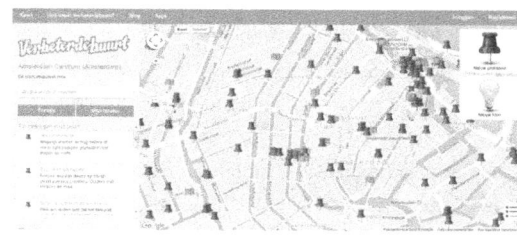

councils, at the moment 320 out of 416 municipalities in the Netherlands accept the Verbeter de Buurt reports and about 20 of them have a customized package to streamline these reports. Verbeter de Buurt is technically licensing their software to Perfect View, a company that handles the majority of the back end systems of municipal councils. As several highly sensitive processes go through these systems, they are very complicated and the team of Verbeter de Buurt is too small to manage them efficiently. So Perfect View will make sure that councils do not receive e-mails with reports but that reports will be automatically incorporated in their regular workflow. This will be both smoother for the municipal employees and will allow Verbeter de Buurt to focus on the user experience of the application. Their main goal is to put forward the ideas instead of the complaints and motivate the people to get together to realize them.

The organization prides itself on being completely independent and feels that their way of working can be more valuable on a larger scale as well. Municipalities should not constantly have to create their custom-made tools, they should embrace solutions and initiatives that are already out there.

## AWARENESS CAMPAIGNS & DESIGNING GOVERNANCE FRAMEWORKS

Verbeter de Buurt is primarily user oriented and tries to balance expectations by not making its interface too game-like or exaggerating. People should not expect to improve the world by using Verbeter de Buurt, but it should make them feel like they are contributing to their area's livelihood and wellbeing. In that sense, it also acts as a successful campaigning tool for local engagement. The interface should be friendly, easy to use and attractive, and encourage a personal tone in the presentation of issues by the users. In the case of Verbeter de Buurt, the online platform is the main tool of engaging their audience. They have also developed an iPhone and Android app and they maintain a blog on the website where they highlight specific ideas that they consider promising and follow their development. As part of their community management Verbeter de Buurt also has a Facebook page and Twitter account.

The nature of most issues reported in Verbeter de Buurt is of very local interest. As people do not really care about broken street lights even two streets down the block, there is a lot of effort from the organization to keep the platform both easily accessible on this highly local level, yet nationally relevant as well, as areas may share the same issues and could tackle them collectively. They have tried to customize the platform for each municipality council according to their needs, but they eventually feel that a uniform output strengthens the user trust and allows them to offer better services. There are no plans of expanding in other countries, but the team actively work to improve their platform for the Netherlands.

Verbeter de Buurt is a hackable citymaking project because it practically improves a process traditionally carried out by the government. It also functions as a campaign motivating people to care more about their direct environment, both reporting problems and proposing ideas to improve it. The issues that get reported the most in Verbeter de Buurt are dog poo and traffic safety but strangely enough out of the 10 people who visit the website, only 1 is actually reporting something. The rest just surf around to get informed about what goes on in their neighborhood. When a report is being filed in through the platform or the app, it can take two forms: a complaint or an idea. Once the municipality council receives this report, they have three response options, they can either mark it as closed when the problem is fixed, they can reject it if there is not enough information about it, or they can plan it and provide the information on when the issue has been scheduled.

When an issue is closed, Verbeter de Buurt contacts the reporter, to inform them and ask them to confirm that the issue has indeed been resolved. In this way they can rate the performance of each municipality, based on how fast and successful they respond to the reports. Working with this set of data is particularly sensitive, as city councils compete to erase red spots on their maps, but they also don't want to receive bad ratings from external parties, such as Verbeter de Buurt; this could prompt them to quit working with the platform instead of improving themselves. Verbeter de Buurt started with a big viral promotion on Twitter, which was initially their main communication medium. There is a blog on the website, but it is primarily meant for announcements and highlighting issues that they find interesting or that have received wider attention. Additionally, there is group of avid Verbeter de Buurt-users, who receive special treatment. They function as advocators for the platform; many have convinced their local councils to adopt Verbeter de Buurt and others spread the word to their neighbours. In return Verbeter de Buurt keeps in good contact with them, sends them press releases, flyers and other information material. They are also asked to participate in an annual survey to provide feedback and help improve the platform. The team behind the platform would really like to change the way authorities work and make bureaucracy disappear. They also support open communication and they feel they are contributing to this change. In a way, they are providing a service to the city authorities by showing where they fall behind and actively making them more efficient. In addition, they collect a lot of data that city councils could utilize, they can provide maps locating the areas with the most problems, which reports gather widespread interest and even make priority lists for them.

# FURTHER THOUGHTS

We started this publication with a brief description of the advent of a platform society: a society in which more and more aspects of our lives are mediated through digital media platforms. This could have important repercussions for the way citizens organize themselves socially, politically as well as spatially. On the one hand the rise of these platforms brings along a promise (or more precise: a potential) for the empowerment of citizens, who have all kinds of new tools to organize themselves around issues they deem of importance. At the same time, there is also a risk that these platforms will undermine that very agency, as it could very well be the platform owners that determine the conditions for social organization, setting limits to certain practices, while encouraging others. So, we asked, what opportunities, as well as challenges, does the rise of the platform society pose for an open, democratic process of collaborative citymaking?
We introduced the concept of Hackable Citymaking as a lens that allows us to analyse the process we call citymaking in the platform society. In the first part of this publication we used a number of characteristics of existing hacker cultures as points of departure to discuss the challenges and opportunities of digital media in the process of citymaking. The goal of that exercise was to draw up a list of issues that deserve critical attention in the debate about the role of digital media in urban society. The Manifesto, therefore, resulted in eight Hackable City Research Questions that could serve further academic research, as well as be used as an agenda for the public debate about these developments.

In the second part we looked at a number of concrete practices of hackable citymaking, trying to understand how they employed (amongst others) digital media. Here the goal was to point out a number of steps and strategies that citizens, designers and policy makers could use in setting up their own hackable city project.

Taken together these two exercises have led us to come to a more schematic understanding of the process of citymaking, as illustrated in the diagram below:

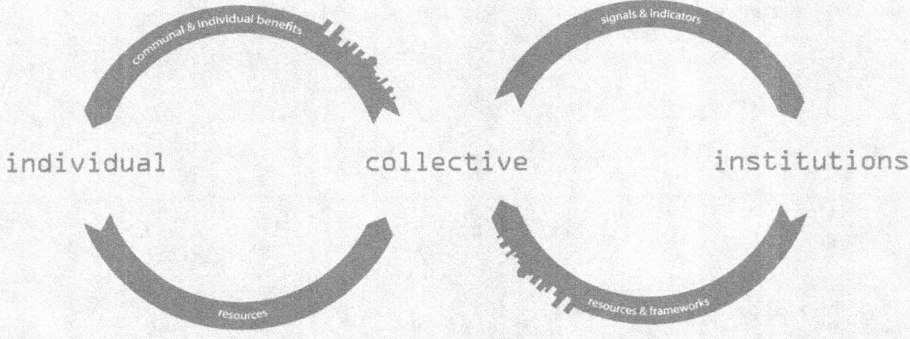

Most instances of hackable citymaking revolve around the organization of individuals in a collective or a public, usually through or with the aid of a digital media platform. Individuals contribute resources, such as knowledge, time, information or money. and at the same time reap some form of a benefit, be it social, economic or political, on an individual or communal level. These platforms allow members of a public to discuss issues, identify with other people or with a common goal, learn from each other, share resources, ideate and act together. They allow for the bundling of individual interests into communal goals or action. Or the other way around: these platforms could provide incentives for individuals to contribute to collective or even public interest goals, organizing publics around a commons.

Much of our research so far has been dedicated to the circle on the left side of the diagram, as we have described seven phases in the hackable citymaking process while singling out eight strategies that are often used in hackable citymaking practices.

At the same time, as we have described in our research manifesto, these collectives or publics do not operate in a social vacuum. They operate within legal and democratic frameworks, sometimes making use of resources of the city at large. One of the main research questions around hackable citymaking is how this relationship between collectives and institutions can be made interactive. How can the governing and administrative institutions of the city open up their infrastructures so that these collectives can improve upon them? How can legal frameworks or administrative practices be opened up to allow for these collectives to shape the city? As we have seen in the research manifesto, an iterative 'tactical urbanism' may be an approach for this, in which collectives start out with a process of small interventions to demonstrate their viability, hoping to convince institutional actors to take them on and make them more permanent. Whereas these collectives can empower a particular group of people to reach a communal goal, this practice also raises the question of inclusion and exclusion as well as the democratic justification of these goals. While we have briefly addressed these issues in our research manifesto, so far we have given them only limited attention in our analysis of hackable citymaking practices. This 'governance' aspect of hackable cities should be an important aspect of future research into this area.

· · · · · · · · ·

Most instances of hackable citymaking revolve around the organization of individuals in a collective or a public, usually through or with the aid of a digital media platform

· · · · · · · · ·

Another core issue in the debate about hackable citymaking lies right in the centre of the diagram: the collective. How and by whom is this public organized? Who owns these platforms and sets their conditions? From what we have learned from our research, there currently is a fuzzy landscape of citizen initiatives, start-up companies and institutional pilot projects that take on this role, often with a central role for designers or architects as central organizers and campaigners, either from their business practice or in a more difficult to categorize role as 'citizen-professionals'.

In future research it's important to form a better understanding of these organization models and their business models. After all, hackable citymaking does not mean that all citizens have to become hackers, devoting their free time to a higher common good. Neither does it mean that all amateurs suddenly can become experts in any domain if only they make use of digital platforms. Hackable citymaking is in need of economic models to run collectives and incentivize individual contributions, and these economic models can take many forms, with the idea of a civic economy as a promising perspective. Likewise, hackable citymaking is about organizing expertise in a self-learning system, and again professional experts could play an important role by contributing their expertise. Not accidentally, many of the projects we have studied are initiated by, or at least include, design professionals that have created tools to engage larger audiences around common issues of concern. Partly motivated by the economic crisis, they have started to look for other roles and positions, either as small-scale developers, as in the case of Buiksloterham, or as urban farmers and entrepreneurs, like Farming the City, or mediators and facilitators in novel civic processes, like Makers+co and Join the Pipe. Like this, they constitute a new type of citymakers that contribute to cities that are open and can be hacked.

In short, for us hackability is a promising lens to explore urban design practices. It's not a panacea for all urban evils or social problems. On the contrary, the practice of hacking the city could be problematic in itself. Yet it is also a concept that helps us to investigate new practices of citymaking that could contribute to more resilient, innovative and liveable cities.

# REFERENCE LIST

Allwinkle, S., & Cruickshank, P. (2011). Creating smart-er cities: An overview. *Journal of Urban Technology, 18*(2): 1-16.

Baccarne, B., Mechant, P., Schuurma, D., De Marez, L., & Colpaert, P. (2014). Urban socio-technical innovations with and by citizens. *Interdisciplinary Studies Journal. Special Issue on Smart Cities, 3*(4)

Barlow, W. (1988). Community radio in the US: The struggle for a democratic medium. *Media, Culture & Society, 10*(1): 81-105.

Beck, U. (1992). *Risk society*. Londen: Sage.

Beunderman, J. (2012). *Compendium for the civic economy : What our cities, towns and neighbourhoods should learn from 25 trailblazers*. London: Trancity Valiz in association with Nesta.

Bria, F. (2015). *Growing a Digital Social Innovation Ecosystem for Europe DSI Final Report*. Brussels: European Union.

Castells, M. (2002). The culture of cities in the information age. In: Susser, I, Castells, M. (Eds.), *The castells reader on cities and social theory*. Malden, MA: Blackwell Publishers.

Denning, D. E. (1996). Concerning hackers who break into computer systems. In: P. Ludlow (Ed.), *High noon on the electronic frontier: Conceptual issues in cyberspace*. Cambridge, MA: MIT Press.

Gabrys, J. (2014). Programming environments: Environmentality and citizen sensing in the smart city. *Environment and Planning D: Society and Space, 32*(1): 30-48.

Gordon, E., & Manosevitch, E. (2010). Augmented deliberation: Merging physical and virtual interaction to engage. *New Media & Society,*

Gordon, E., Schirra, S., & Hollander, J. (2011). Immersive planning: A conceptual model for designing public participation with new technologies. *Environment and Planning B, 38*(3): 505.

Greenfield, A. (2013). *Against the smart city (The city is here for you to use Book 1)*. New York: Do Projects.

Hajer, M. (2011). *De energieke samenleving. Op zoek naar een sturingsfilosofie voor een schone economie*. Den Haag: Planbureau voor de Leefomgeving.

Hemment, D., & Townsend, A. (2013). *Smart citizens*. FutureEverything Publications.

Himanen, P. (2001). *The hacker ethic*. New York: Random House.

Hippel, E. v. (2005). *Democratizing innovation*. Cambridge, MA: MIT Press.

Hollands, R. G. (2008). Will the real smart city please stand up? intelligent, progressive or entrepreneurial? *City, 12*(3): 303-320.

Kitchin, R. (2013). Big data and human geography: Opportunities, challenges and risks. *Dialogues in Human Geography, 3*(3): 262-267.

Klooster, I. v. (2013). *Reactivate!: Innovators of dutch architecture*. New York: Trancity Valiz.

de Lange, M., & de Waal, M. (2013). Owning the city: New media and citizen engagement in urban design. *First Monday, 18*(11)

Leadbeater, C., & Miller, P. (2004). *The pro-am revolution: How enthusiasts are changing our society and economy*. London: Demos.

Levy, S. (2001). *Hackers: Heroes of the computer revolution*. New York: Penguin Books.

Lydon, M., & Garcia, A. (2015). *Tactical urbanism: Short-term action for long-term change*. Washington DC: Island Press.

Ratti, C., & Townsend, A. (2011). The social nexus. *Scientific American, 305*(3): 42-48.

Raymond, E. (1999). The cathedral and the bazaar. *Knowledge, Technology & Policy, 12*(3), 23-49.

Roszak, T. (1986). *The cult of information: The folklore of computers and the true art of thinking*. New York: Pantheon Books.

Söderström, O., Paasche, T., & Klauser, F. (2014). Smart cities as corporate storytelling. *City, 18*(3): 307-320.

Tonkens, E., Trappenburg, M., Hurenkamp, M., & Schmidt, J. (2015). *Montessori democratie: Spanning tussen burgerparticipatie en de lokale politiek*. Amsterdam: Amsterdam University Press.

Townsend, A. M. (2013). *Smart cities: Big data, civic hackers, and the quest for a new utopia*. New York: WW Norton & Company.

Turner, F. (2006). How digital technology found utopian ideology. In D. Silver, & A. Massanari (Eds.), *Critical cyberculture studies: Current terrains, future directions*. New York: NYU Press.

Wark, M. (2004). *A hacker manifesto*. Cambridge, MA: Harvard University Press.

www.ingramcontent.com/pod-product-compliance
Lightning Source LLC
Chambersburg PA
CBHW070429180526
45158CB00017B/945